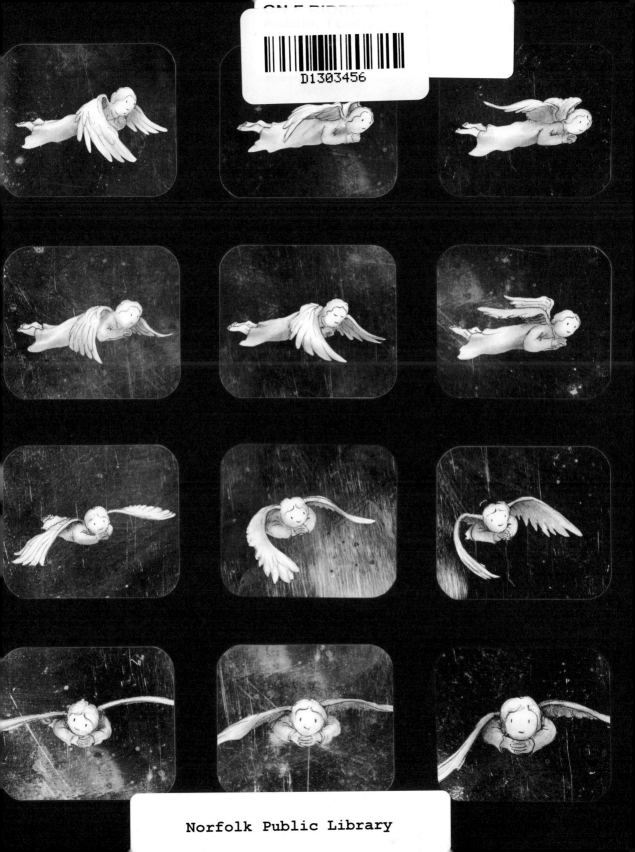

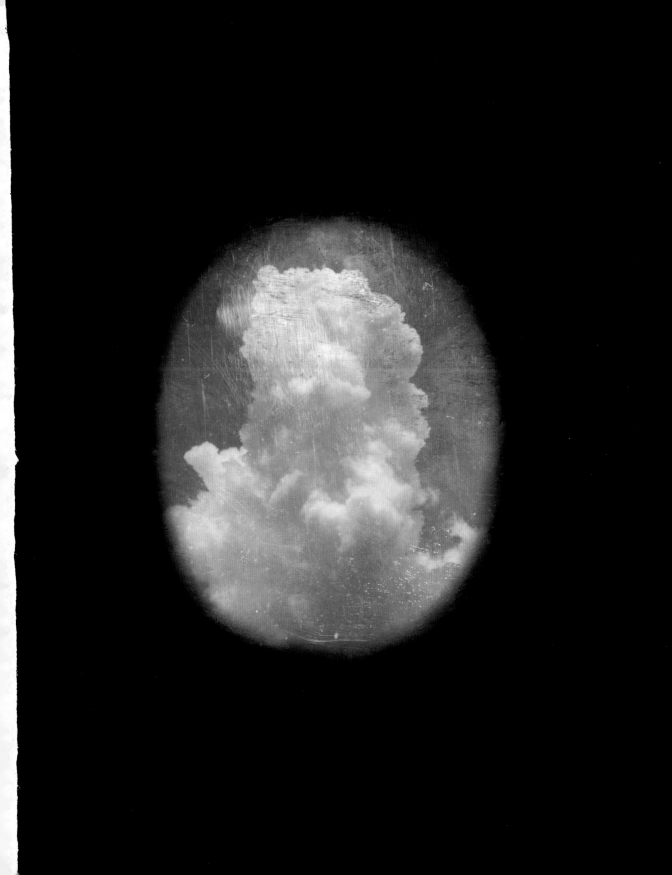

THE BERKLEY PUBLISHING GROUP
Published by the Penguin Group
Penguin Group (USA) Inc.
375 Hudson Street, New York, New York 10014, USA

USA | Canada | UK | Ireland | Australia | New Zealand | India | South Africa | China

Penguin Books Ltd., Registered Offices: 80 Strand, London WC2R 0RL, England
For more information about the Penguin Group, visit penguin.com.

Published by arrangement with Allen & Unwin.

UNFORGOTTEN

InkLit and the InkLit design are trademarks of Penguin Group (USA) Inc.

InkLit hardcover ISBN: 978-0-425-27091-2

An application to register this book for cataloging has been
submitted to the Library of Congress.

PUBLISHING HISTORY
Originally published by Allen & Unwin
InkLit hardcover edition / November 2013

PRINTED IN CHINA

10 9 8 7 6 5 4 3 2 1

Design by Tohby Riddle and Bruno Herfst.

ALWAYS LEARNING   PEARSON

UNFORGOTTEN

Tohby Riddle

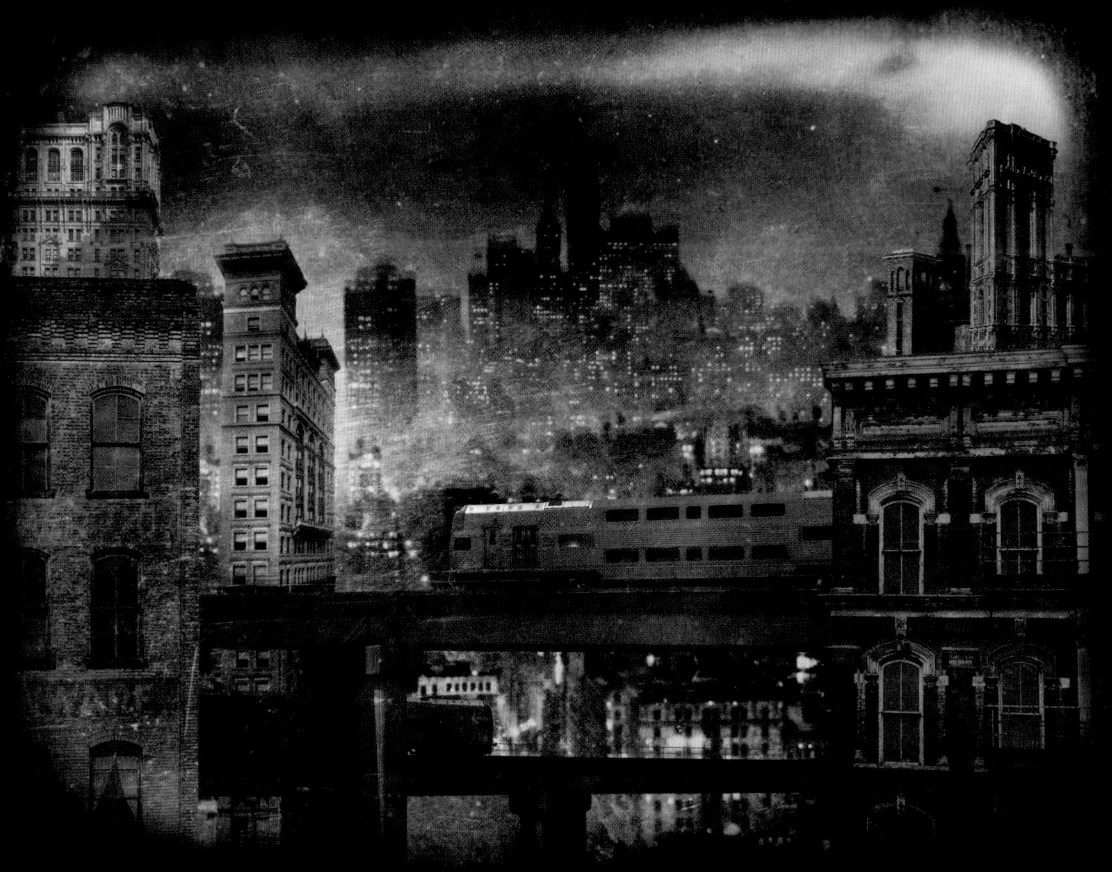

Ink Lit

I

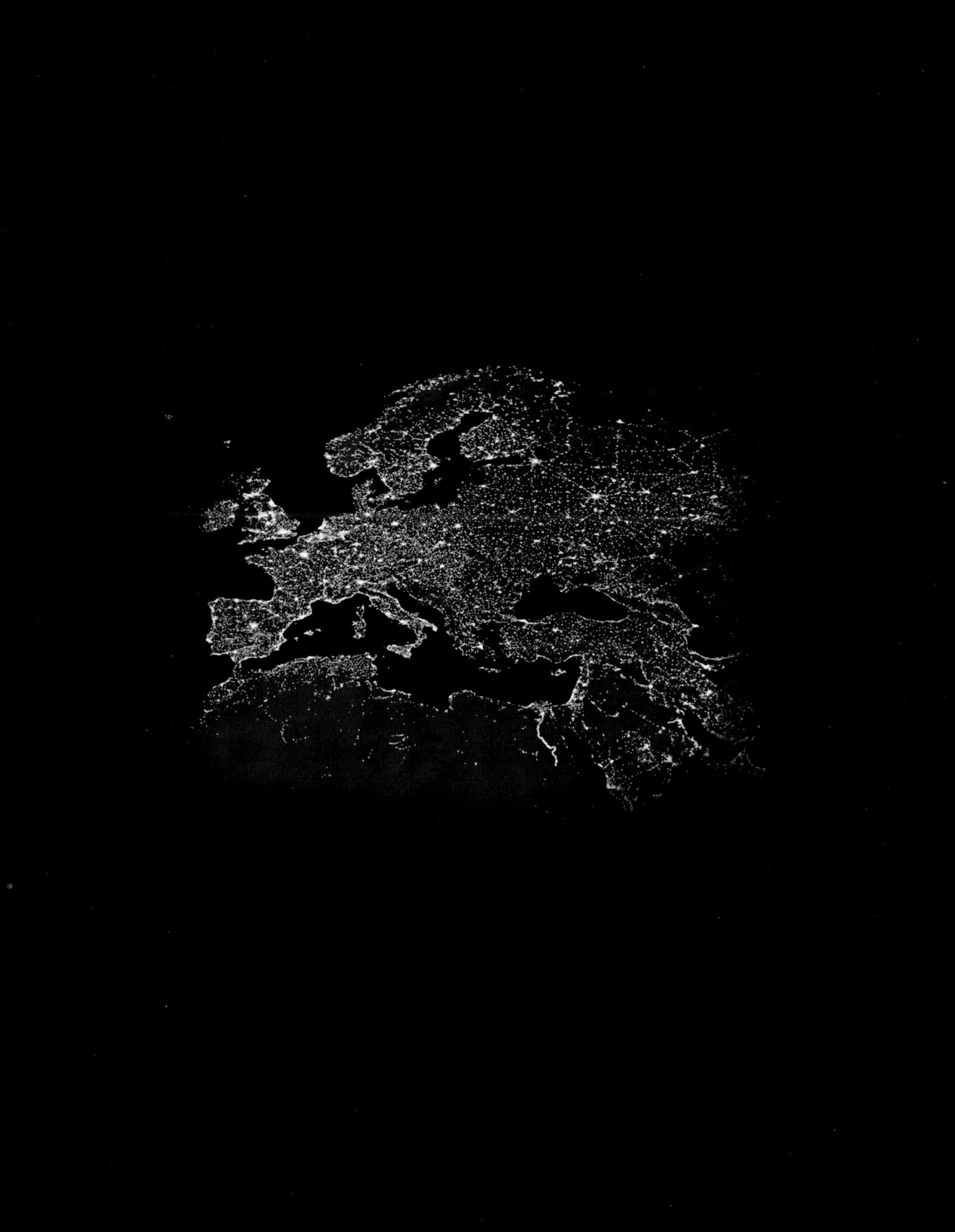

Nobody knows where they come from.

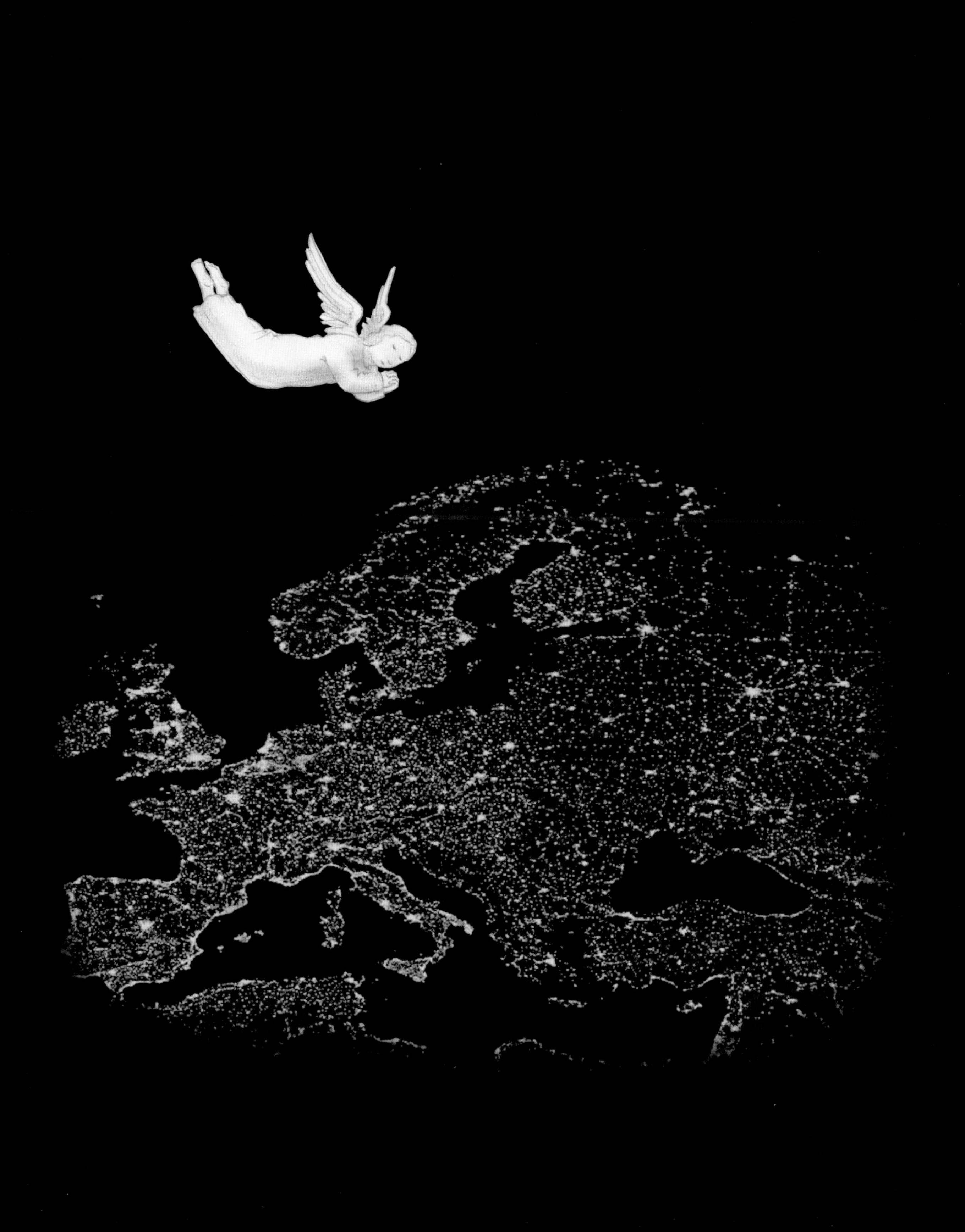

But they come.

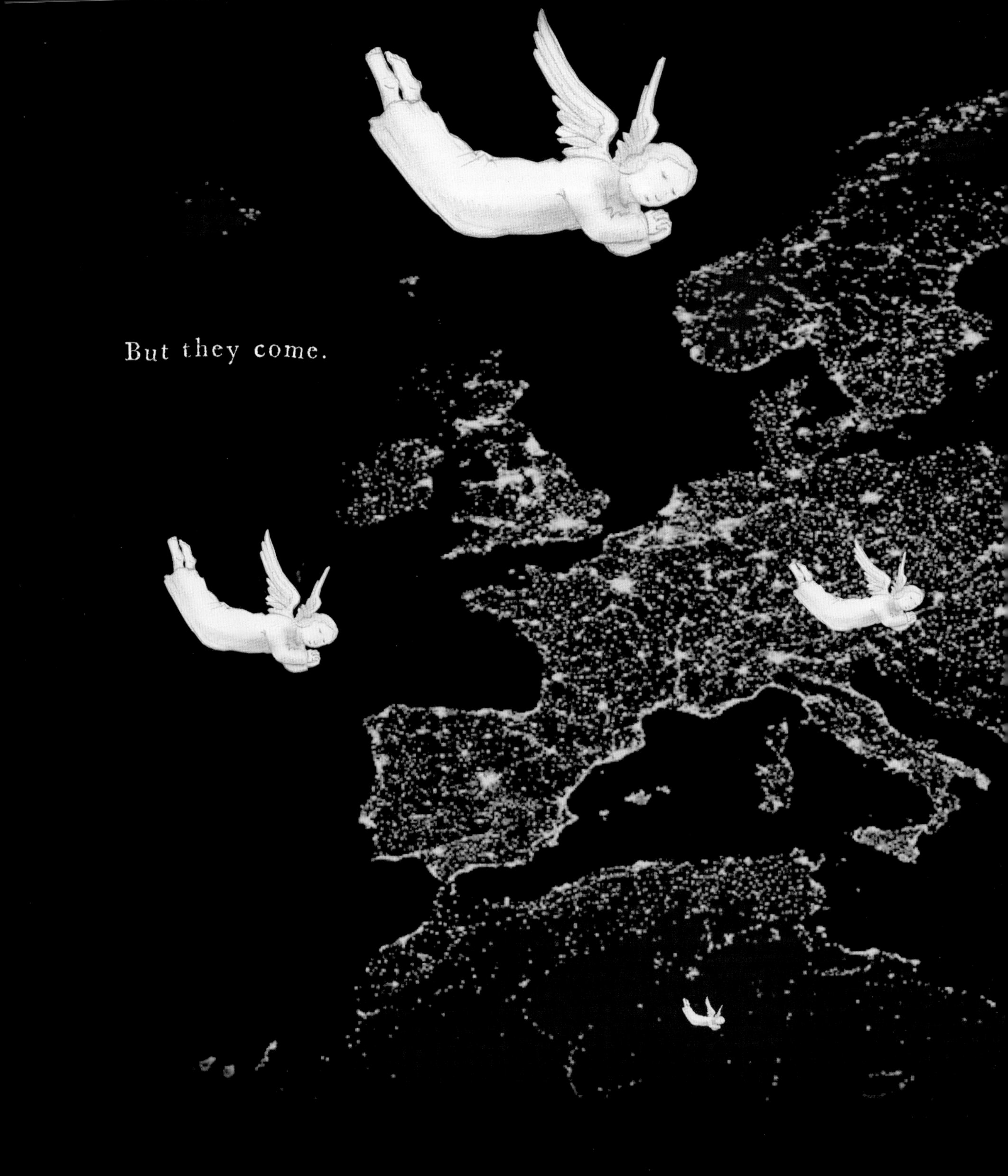

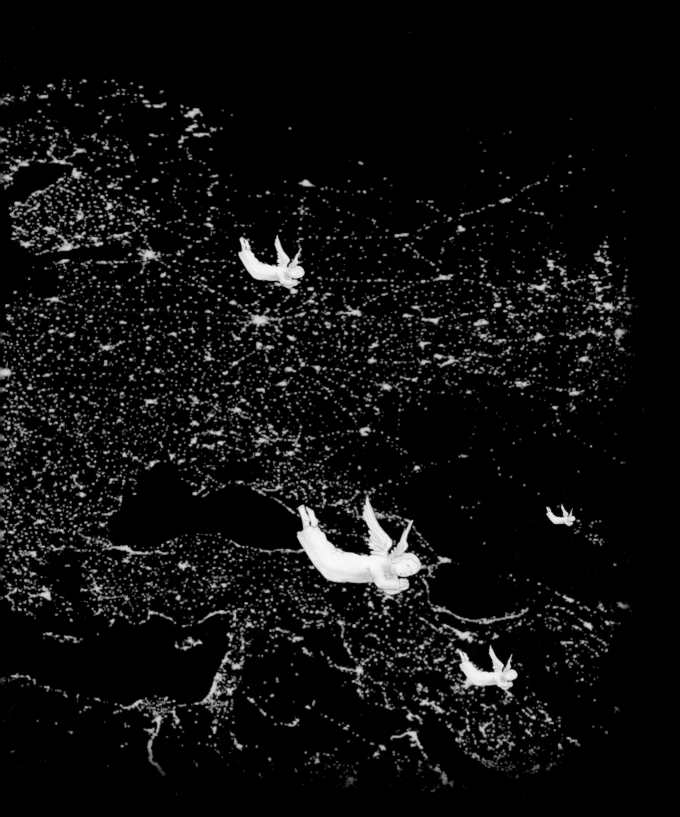

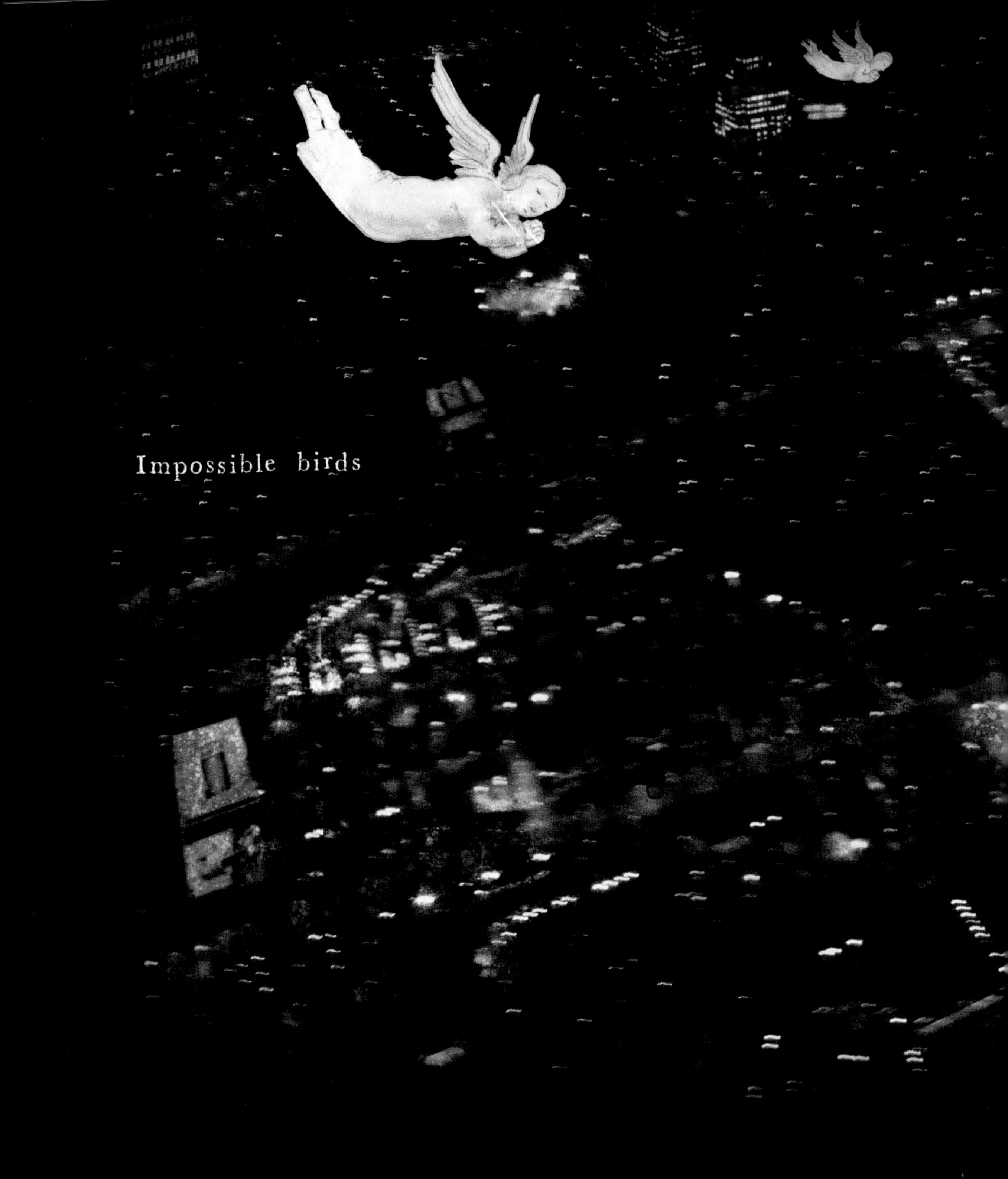

Impossible birds

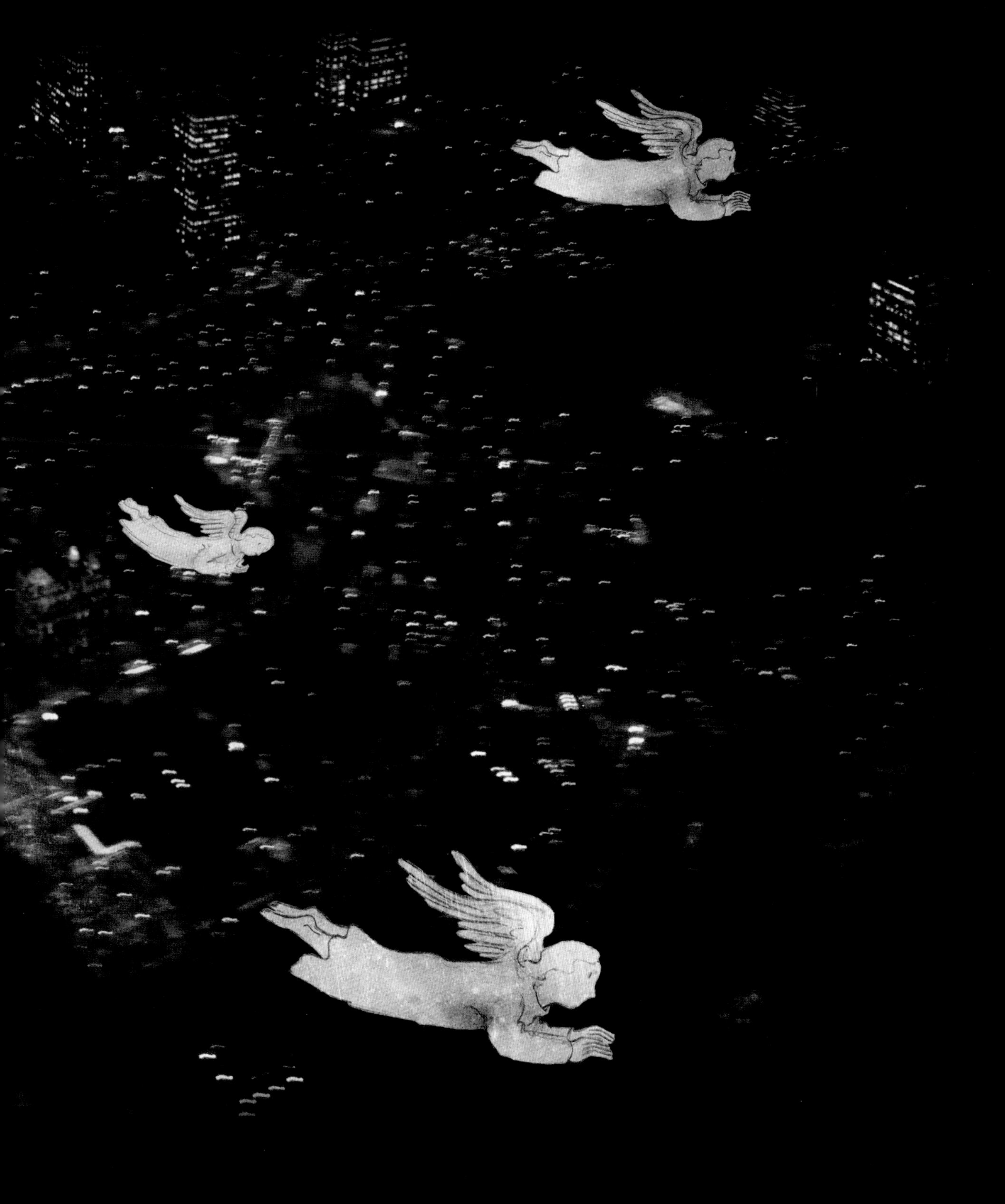

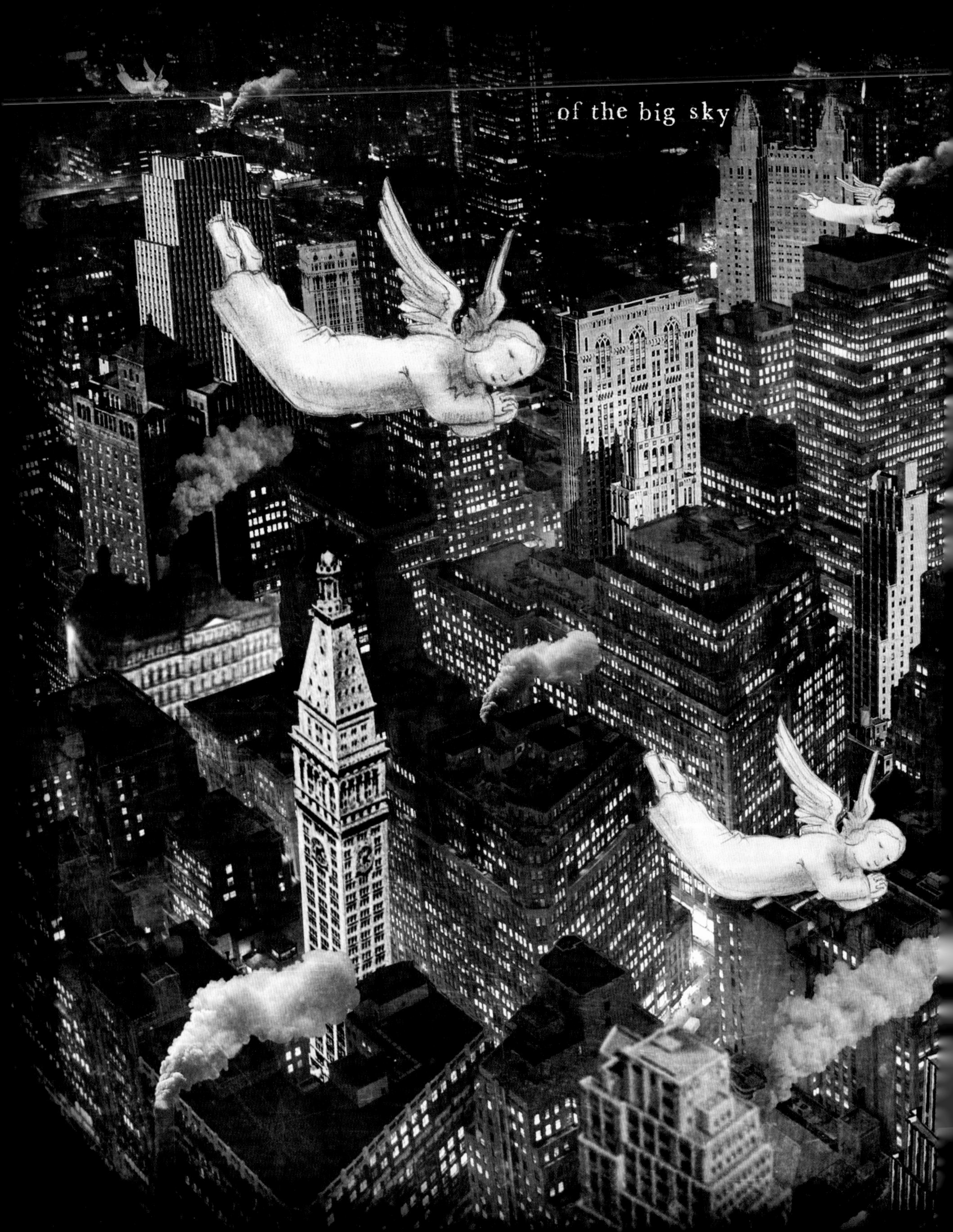
of the big sky

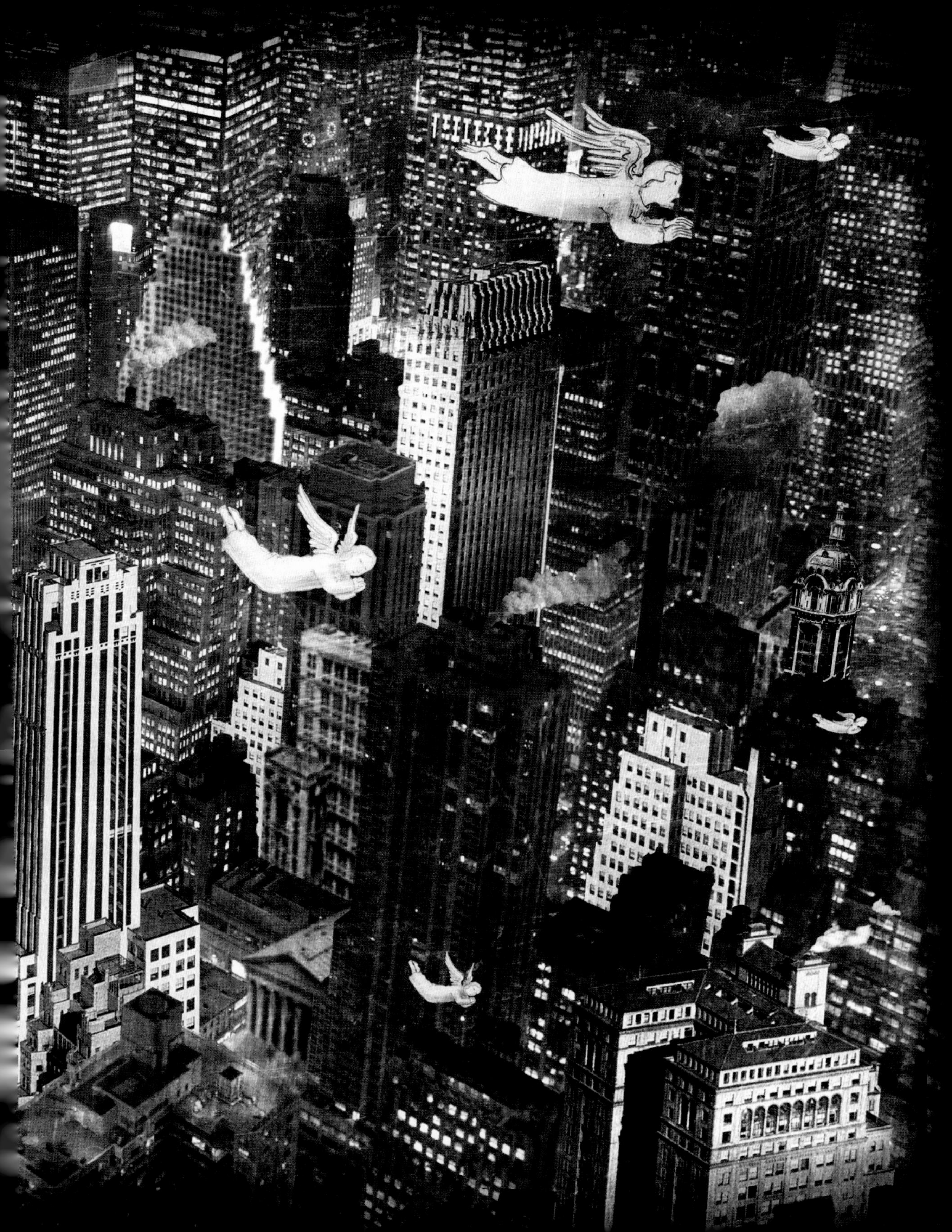

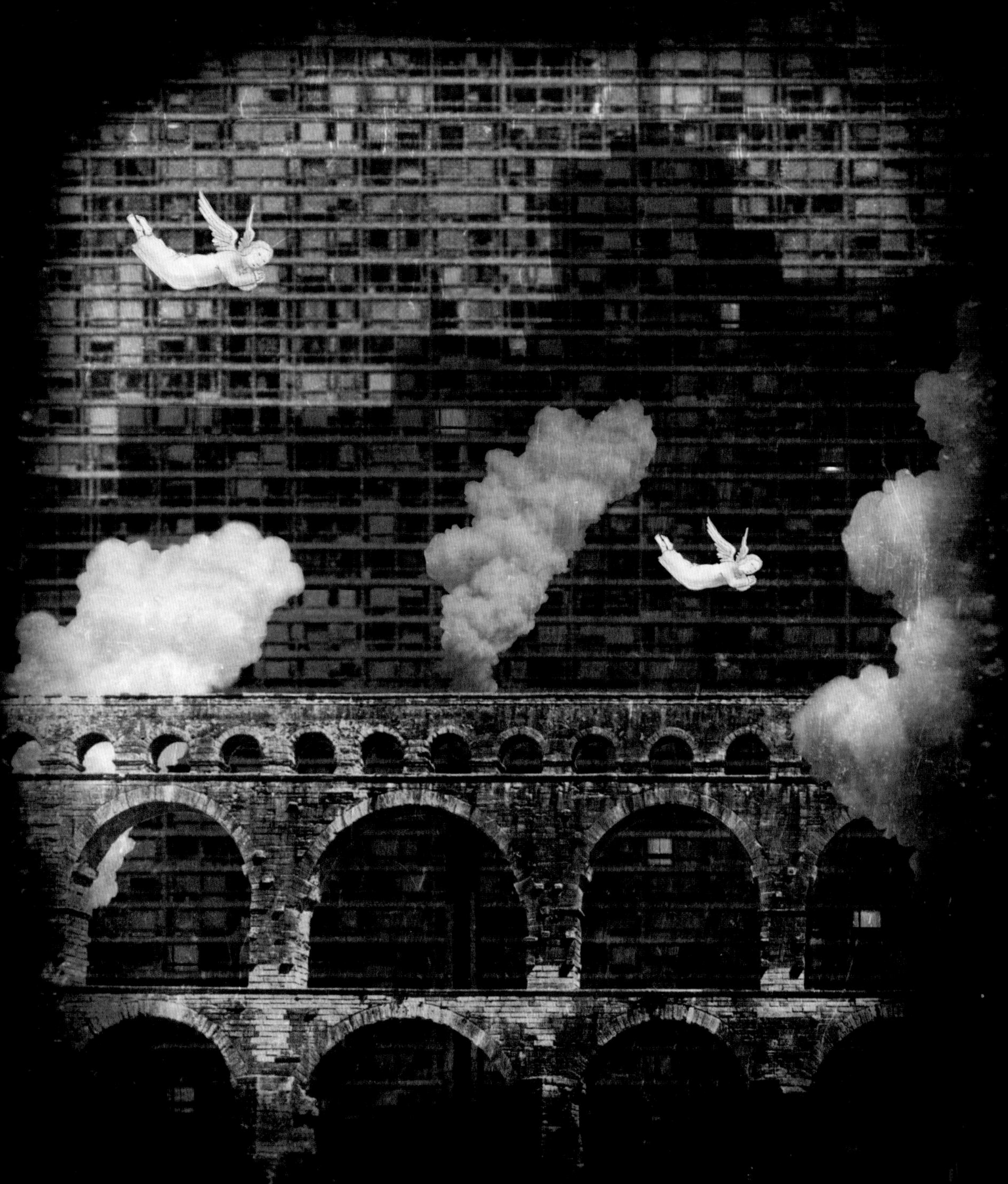

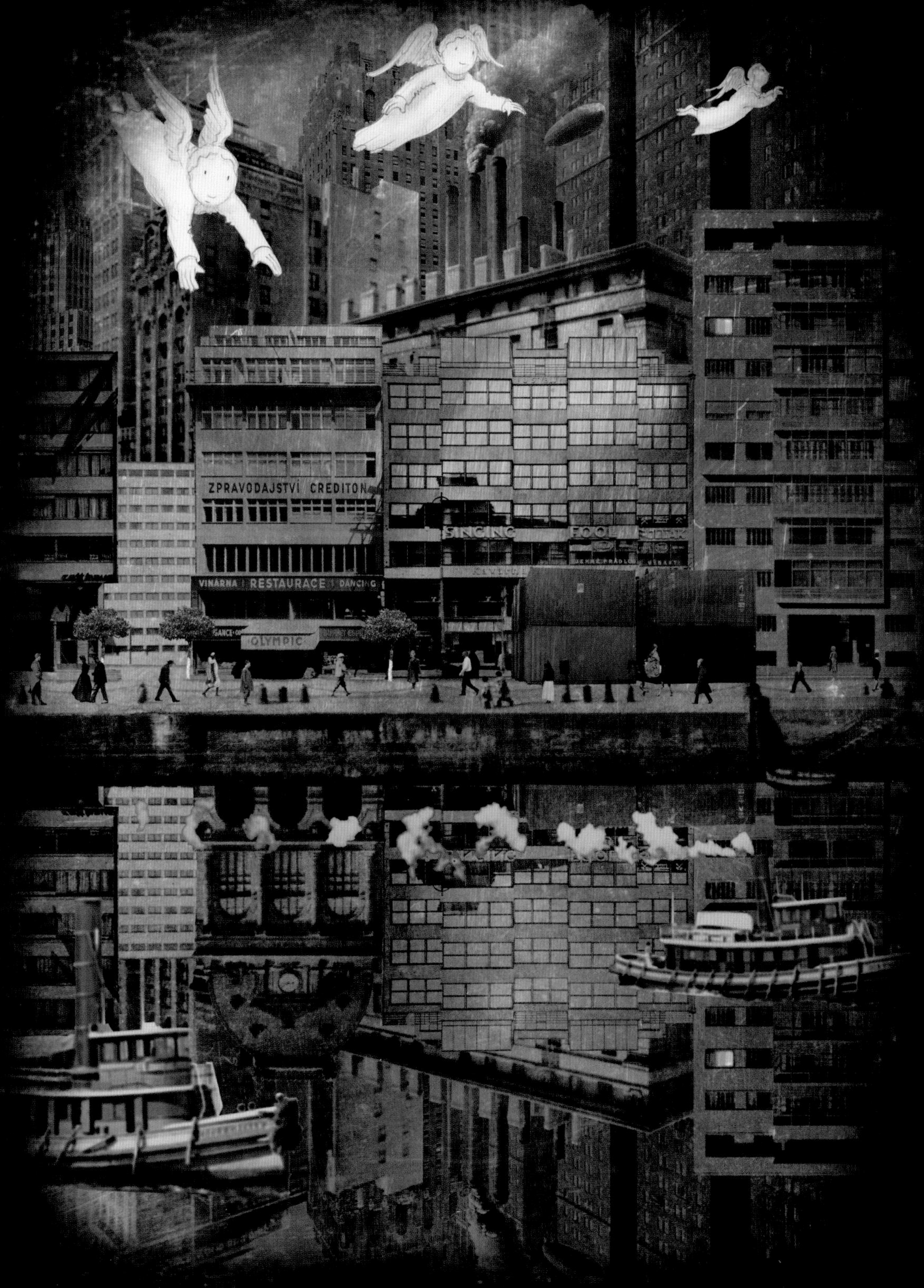
ZPRAVODAJSTVÍ CREDITON
SINGING
FOOL
VINARNA
RESTAURACE
DANCING
OLYMPIC

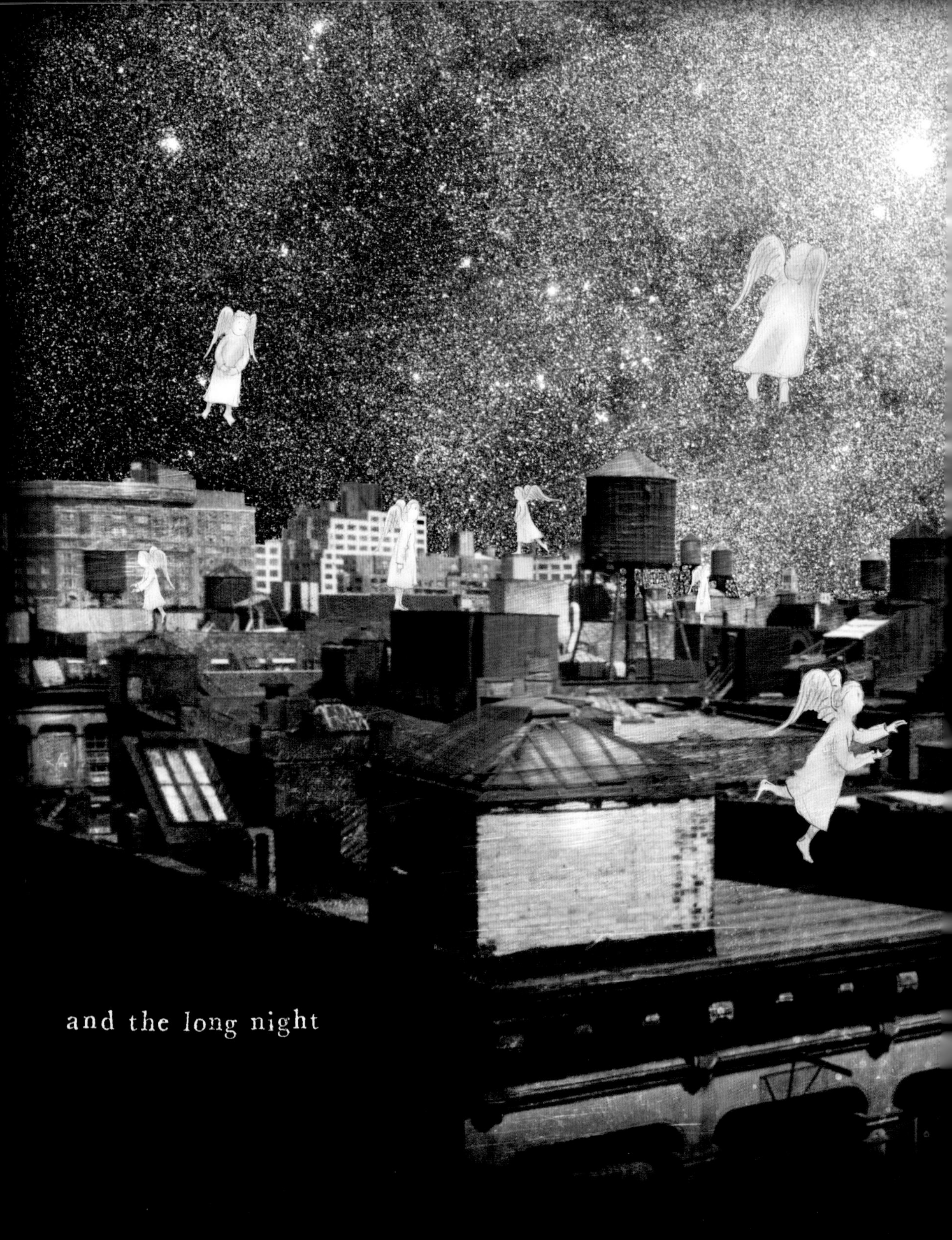

and the long night

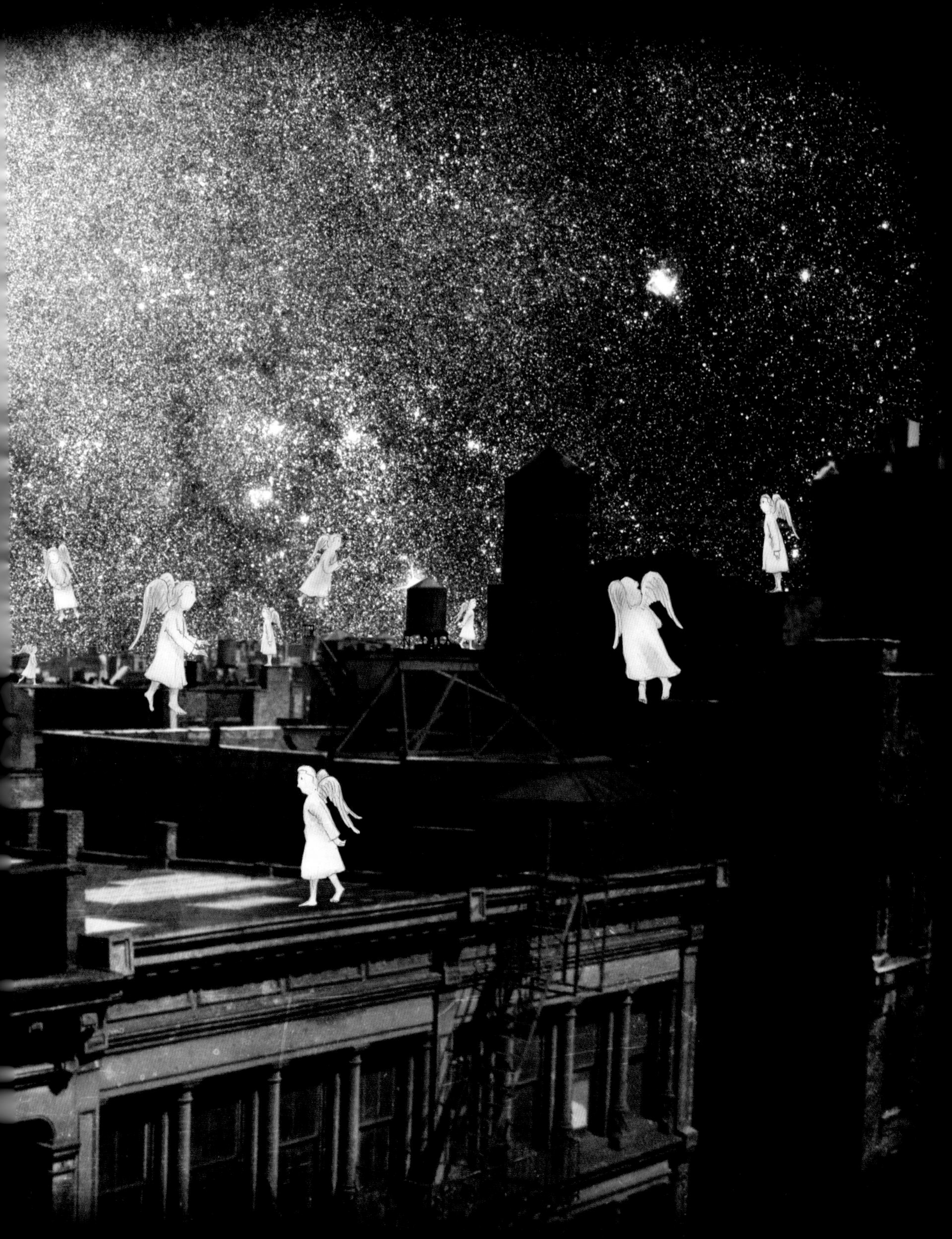

with faintest whispers

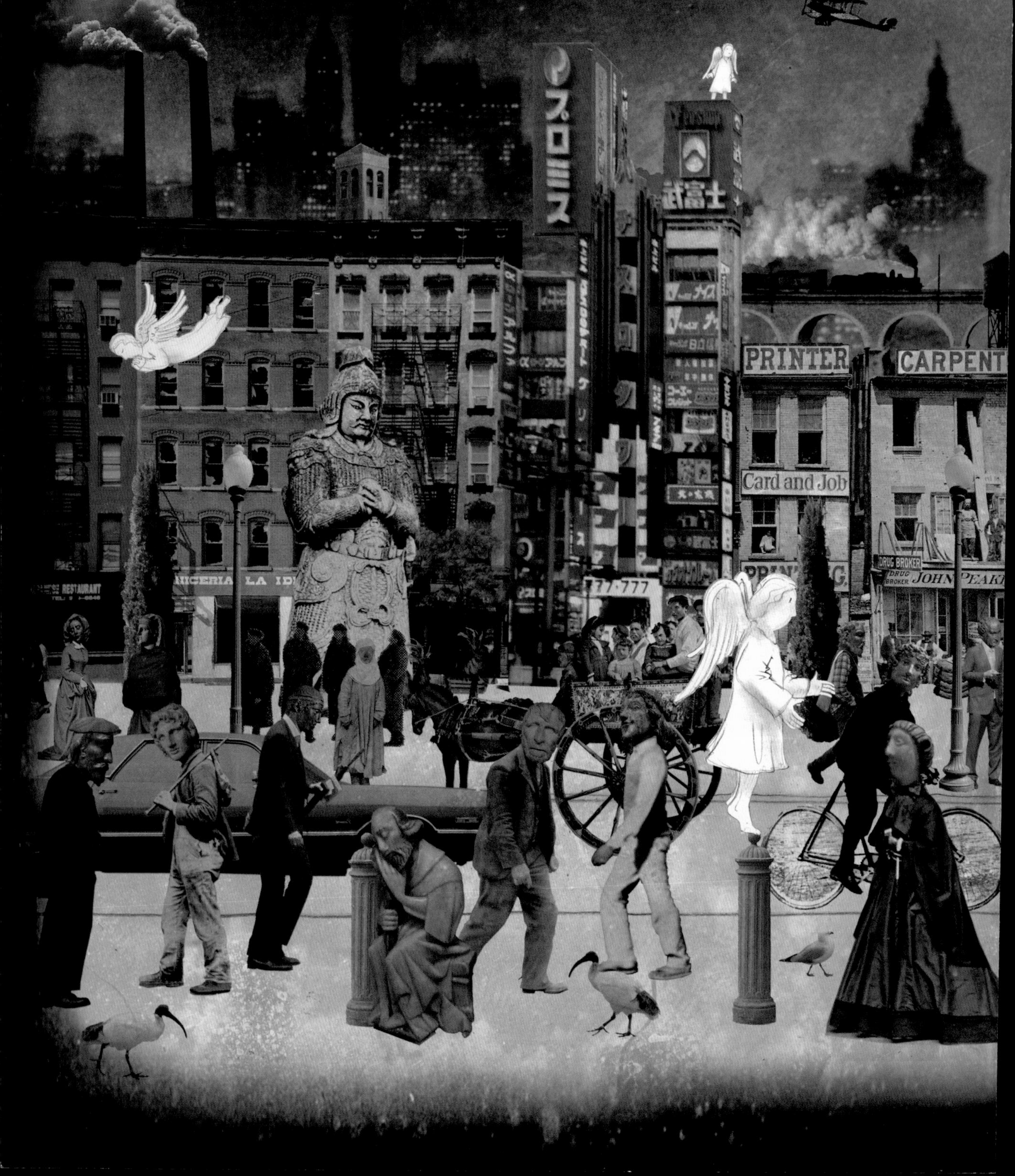
プロミス
武富士
PRINTER
CARPENT
Card and Job
DRUG BROKER
JOHN PEAK
RESTAURANT

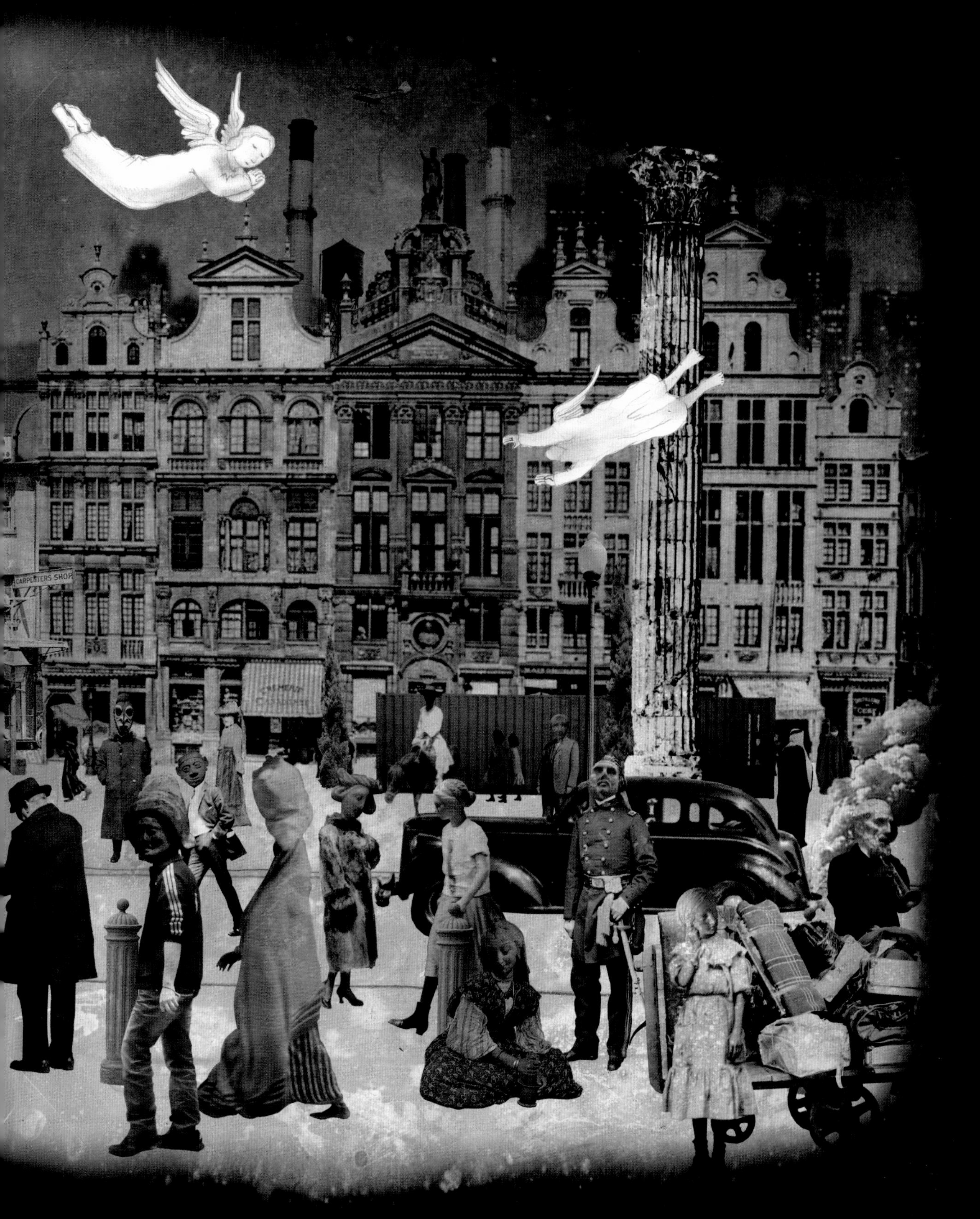
CARPENTERS SHOP

and silky rustlings

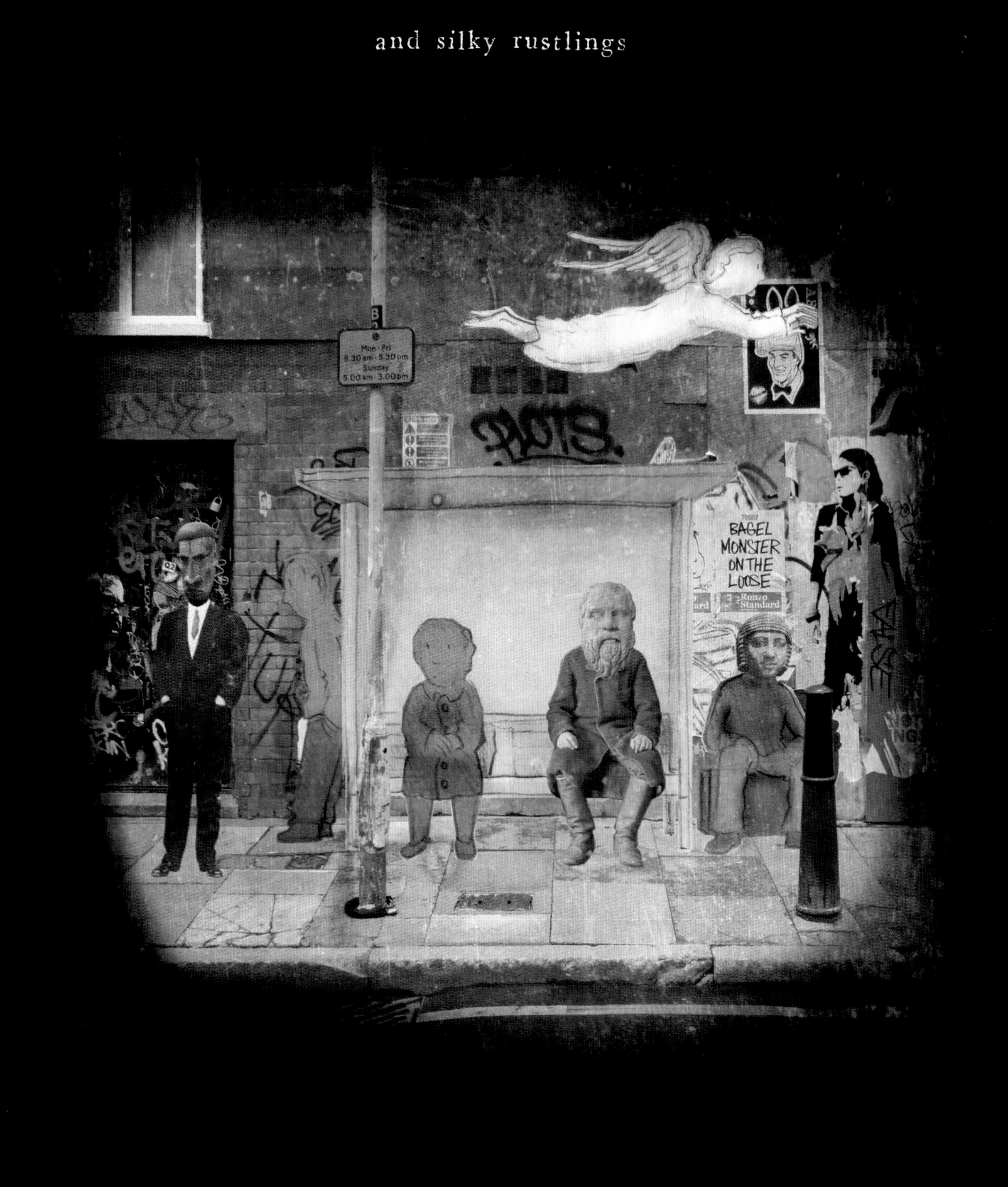
Mon - Fri
8.30 am - 5.30 pm
Sunday
5.00 am - 3.00 pm
TODAY
BAGEL
MONSTER
ON THE
LOOSE
Ronzo
Standard

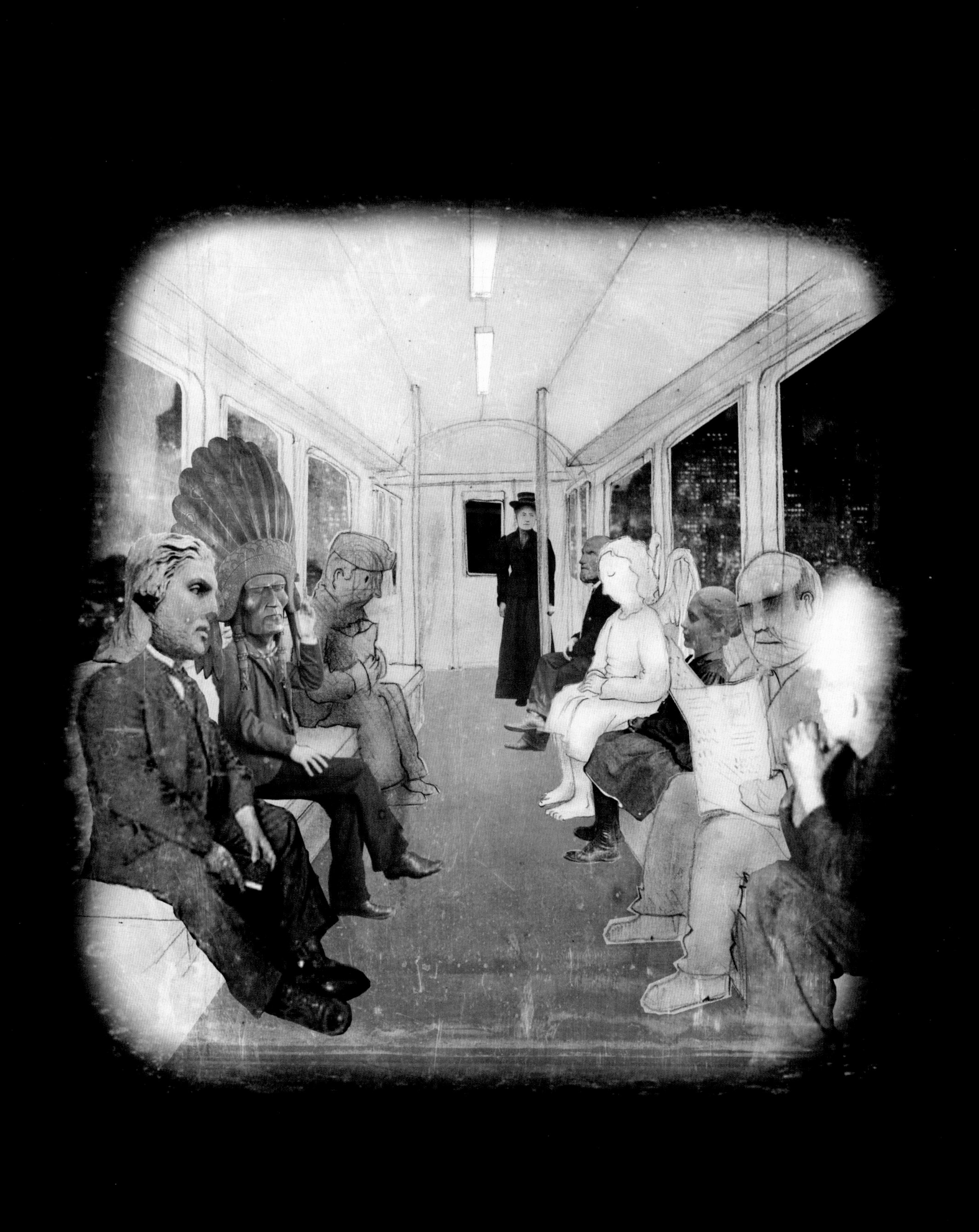

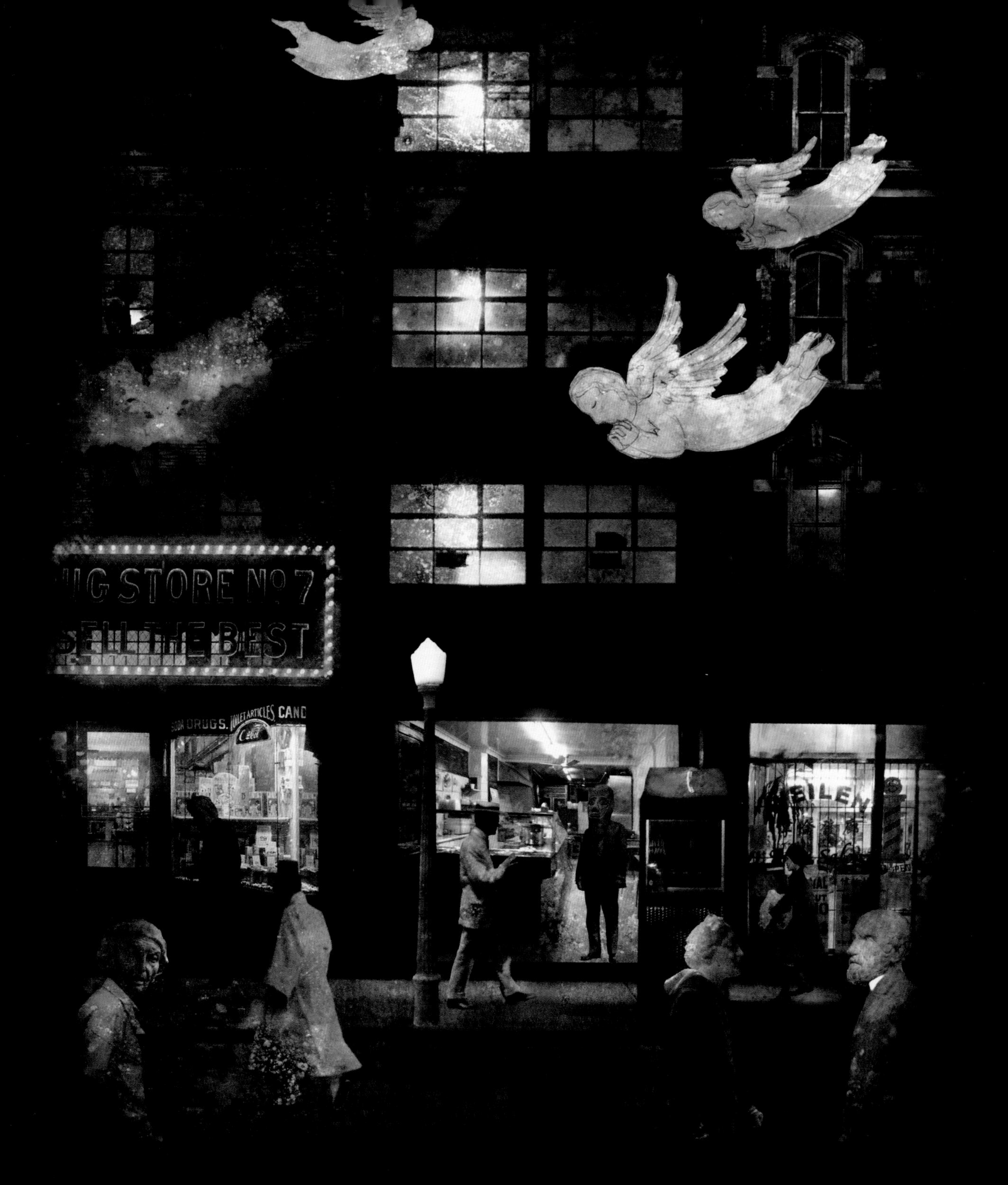
UG STORE No 7
SELL THE BEST
SODA DRUGS. TOILET ARTICLES CAND
EILEN

no ear can hear.

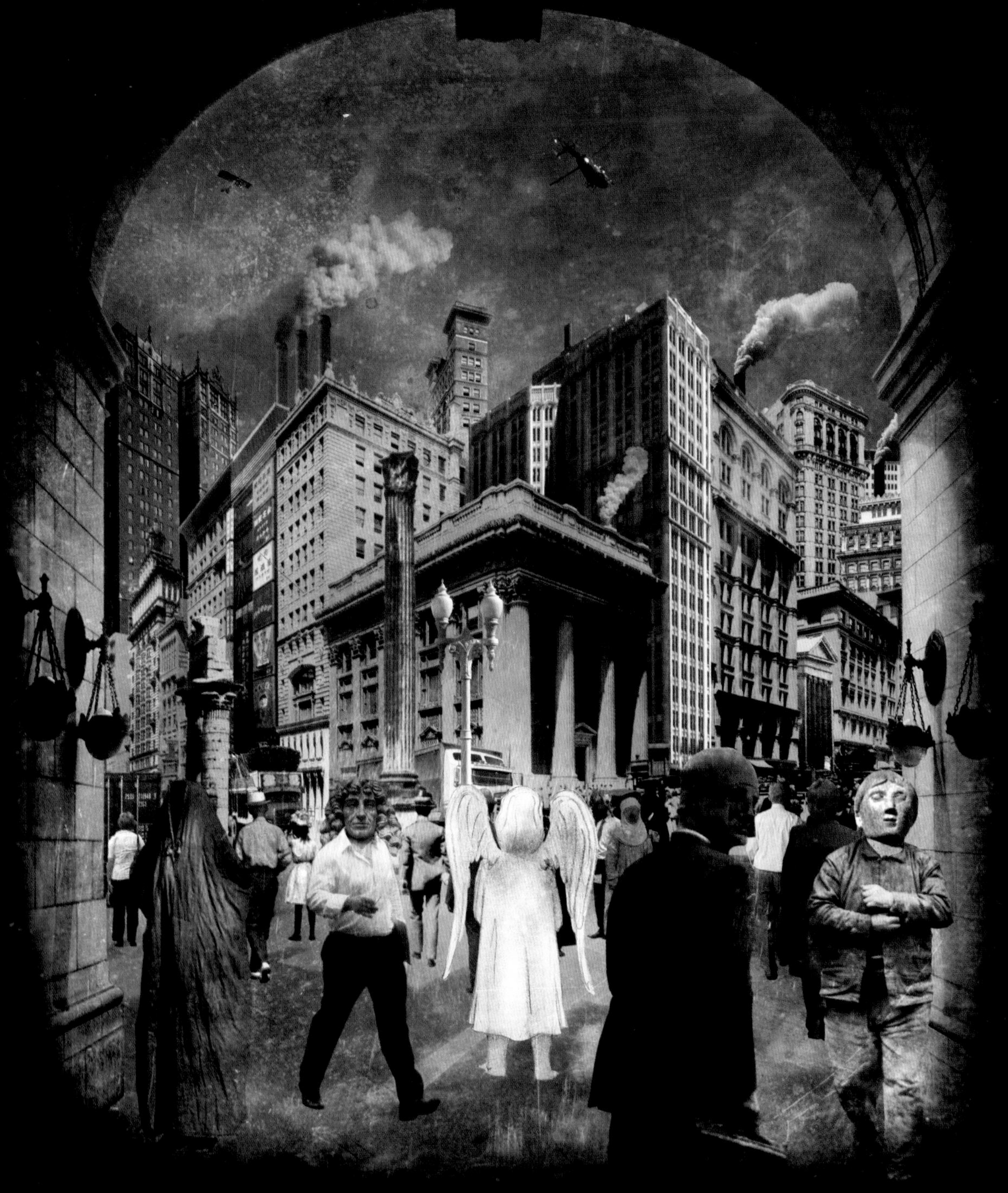

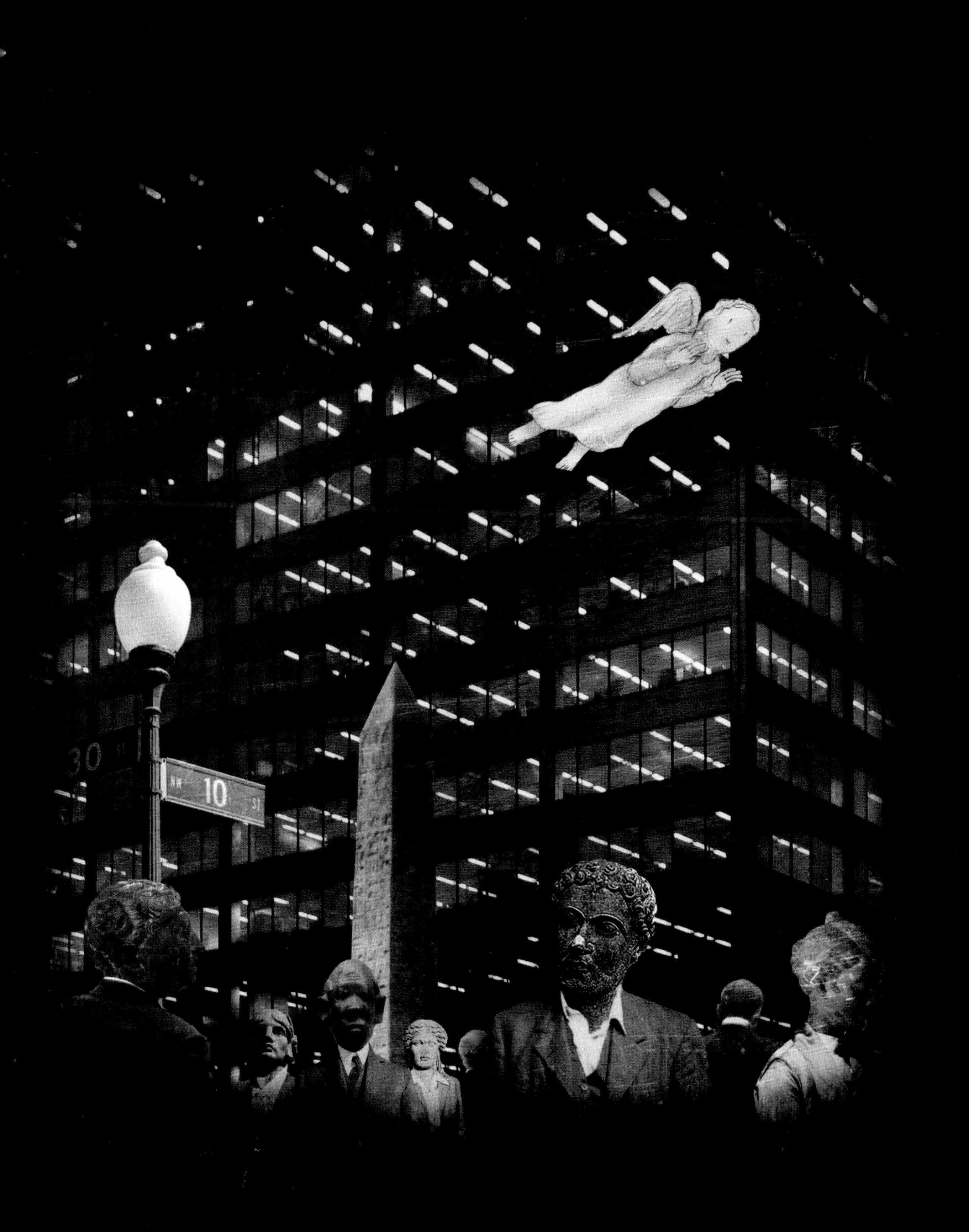
30 ST
NW 10 ST

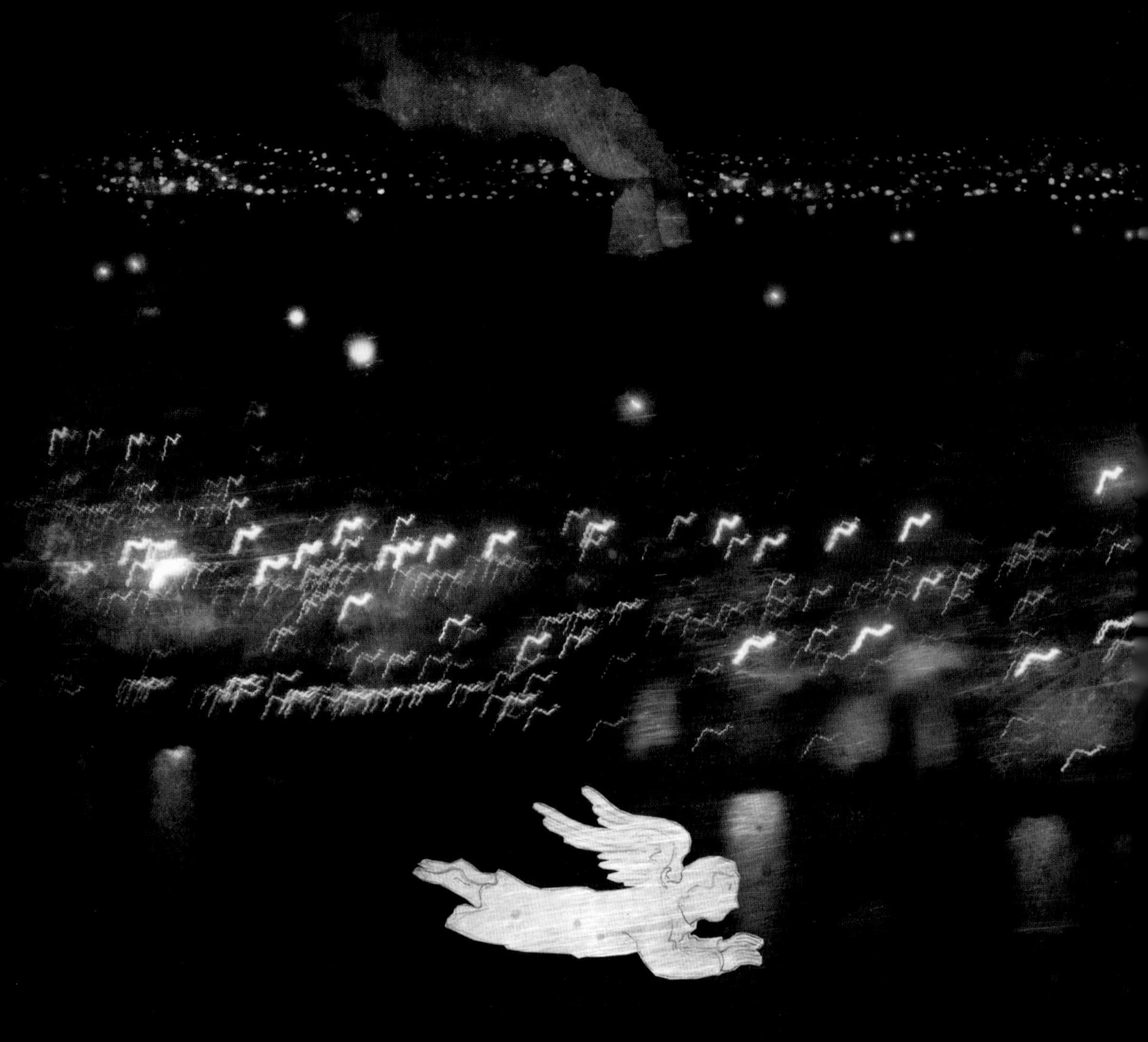

They come

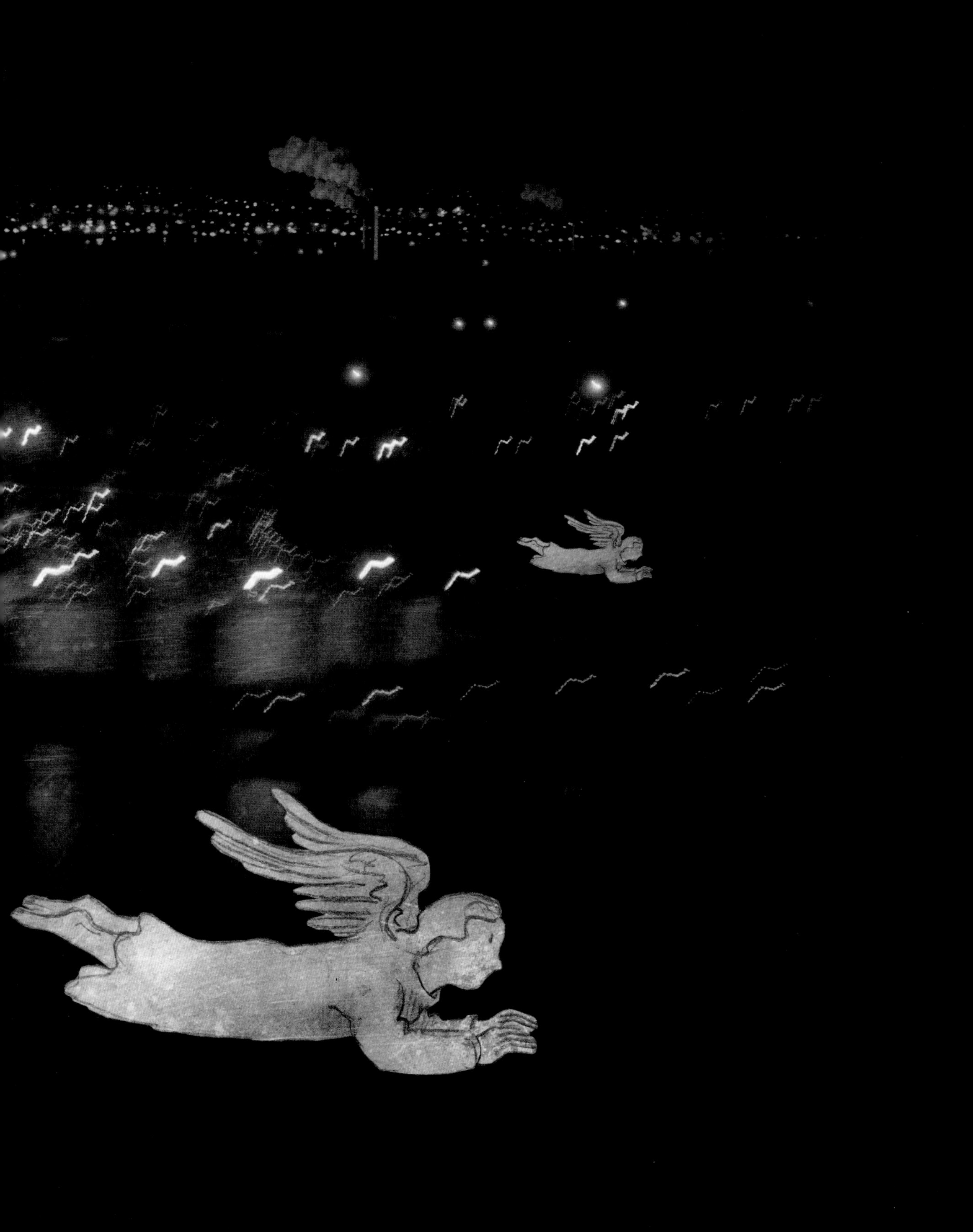

like a flicker

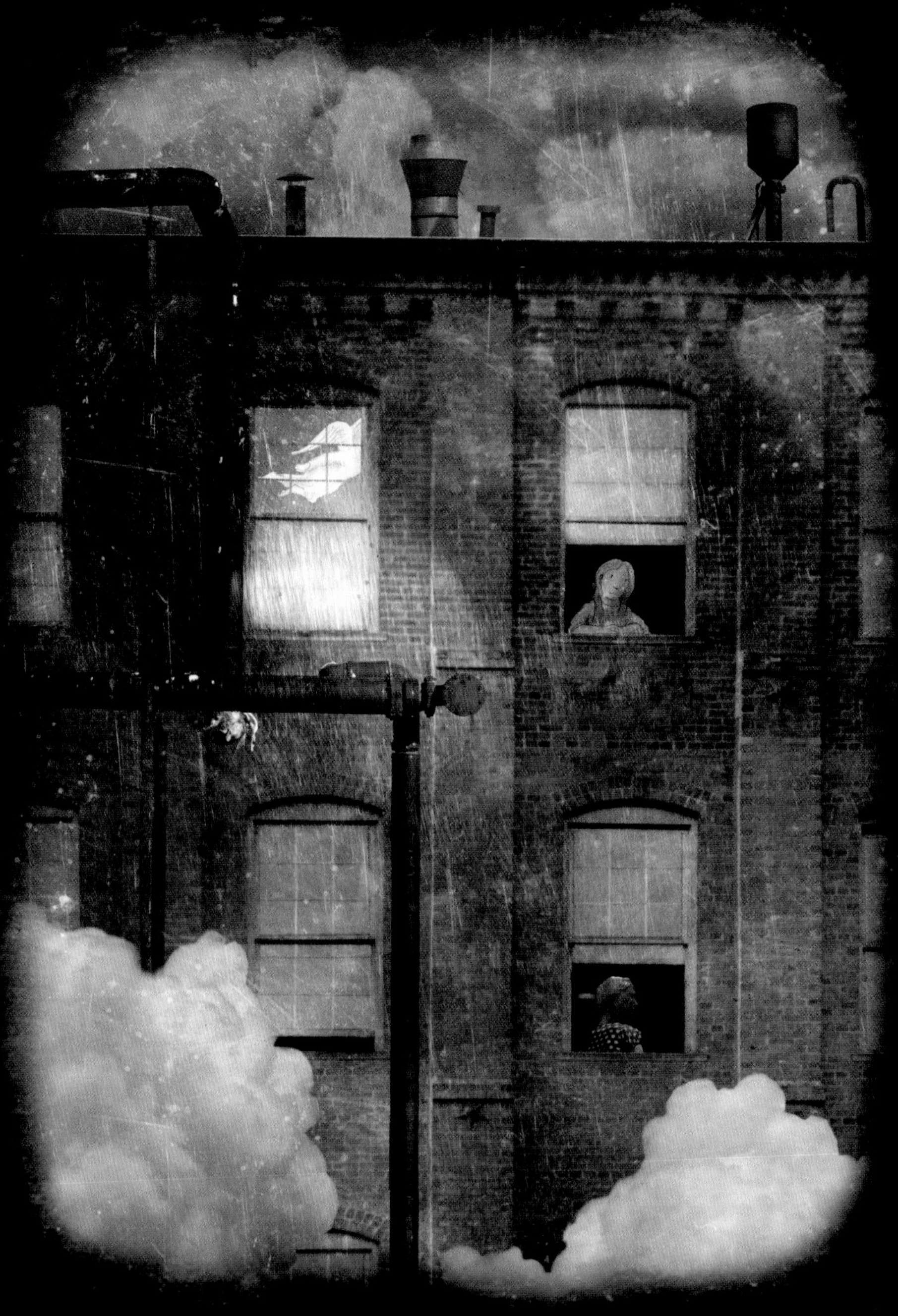

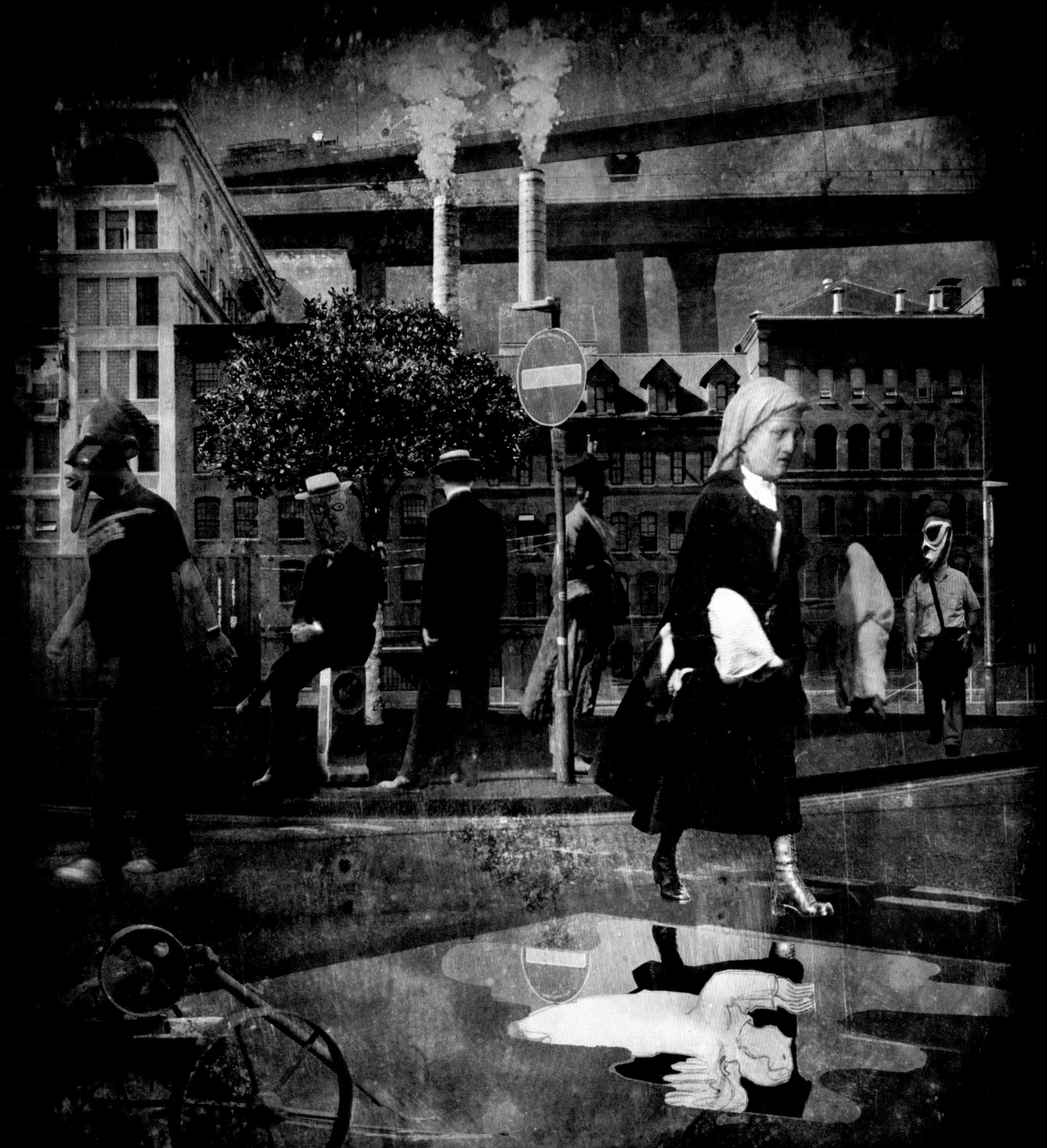

a blink

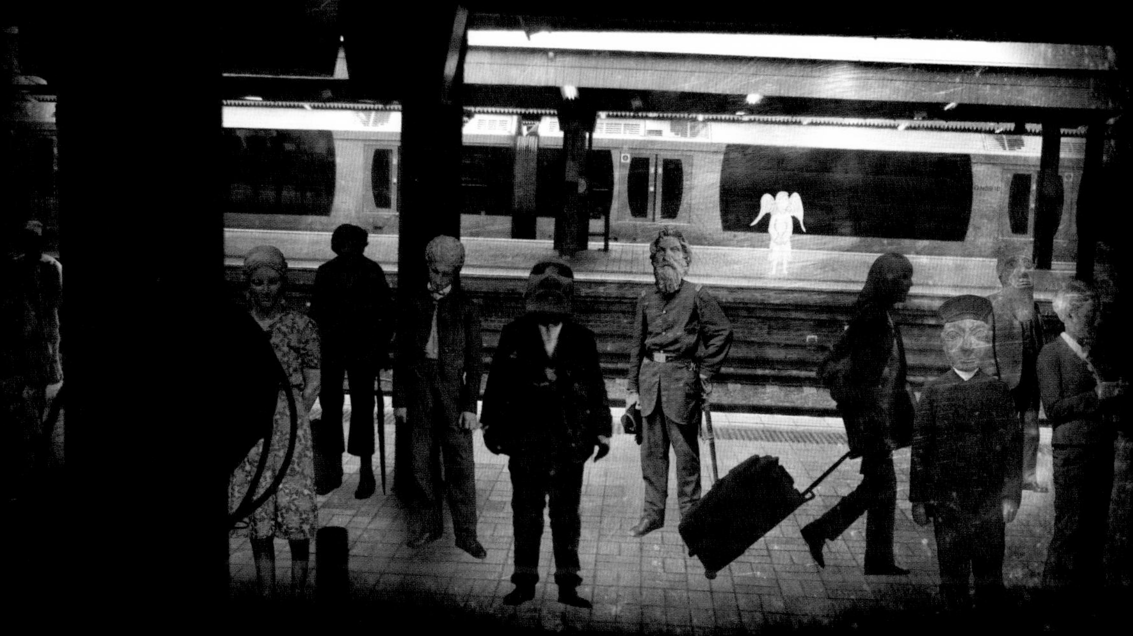

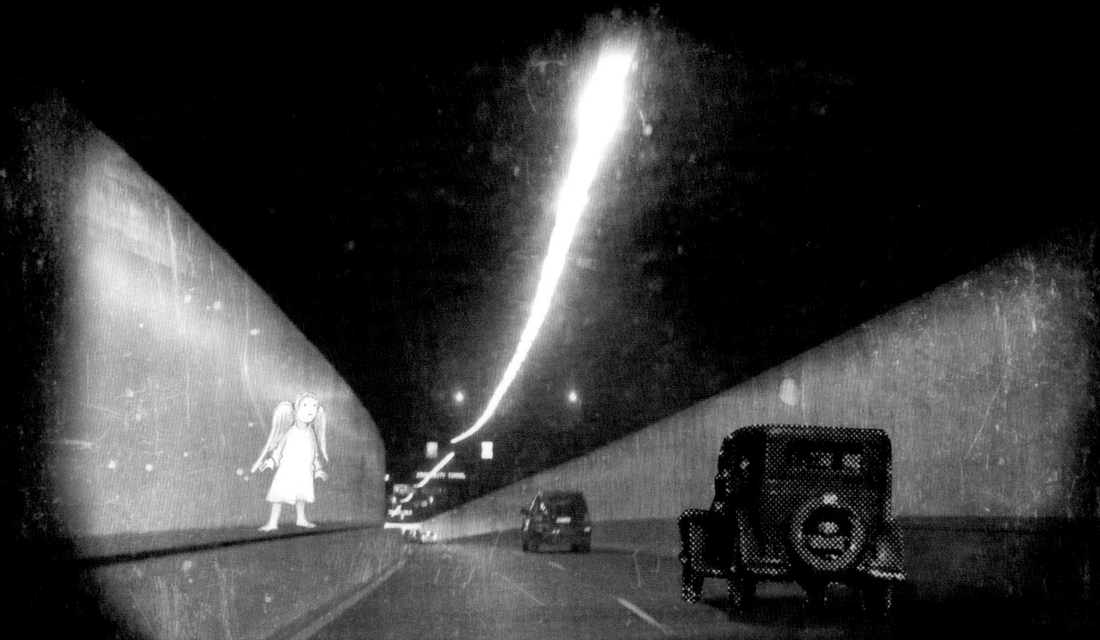

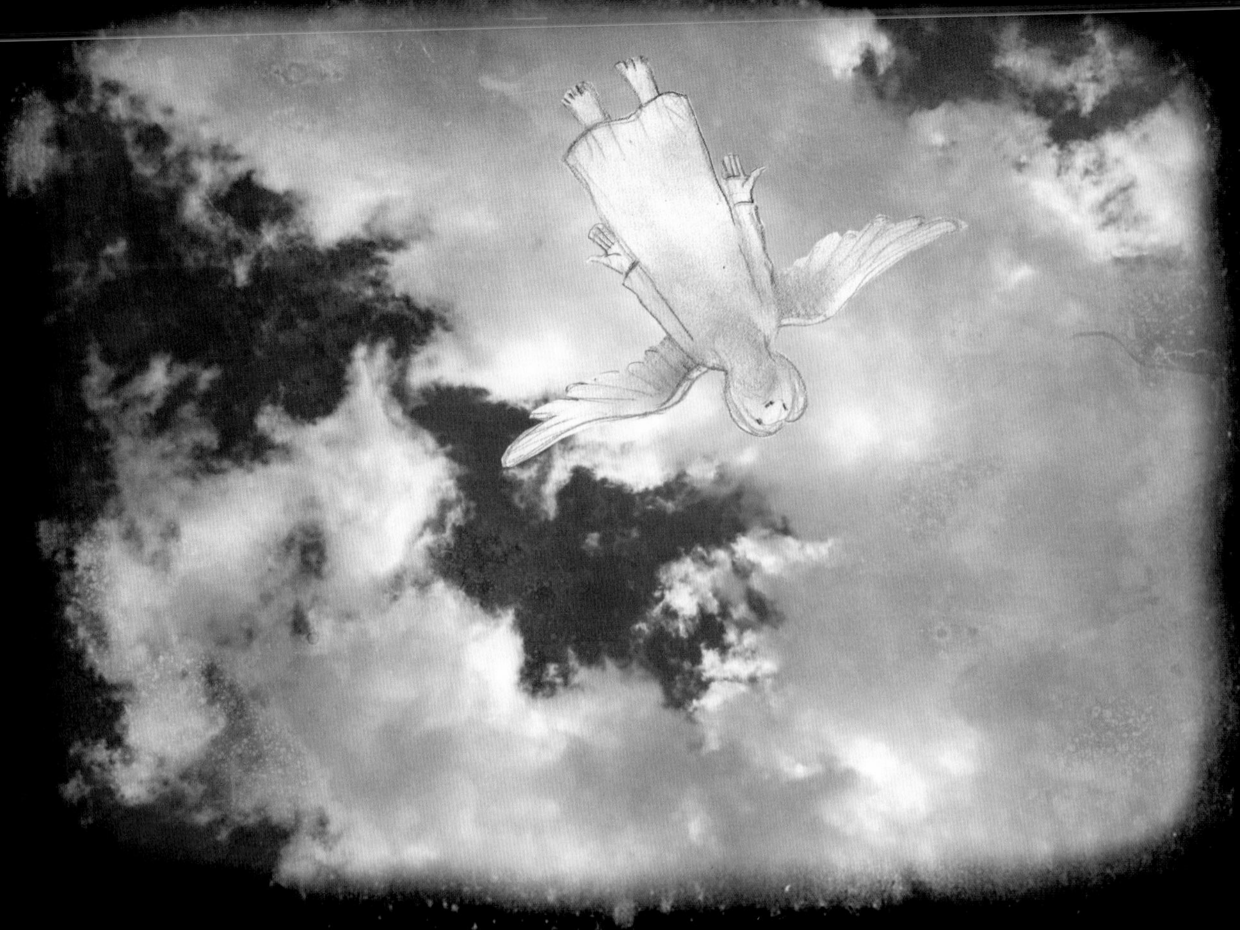

a flash

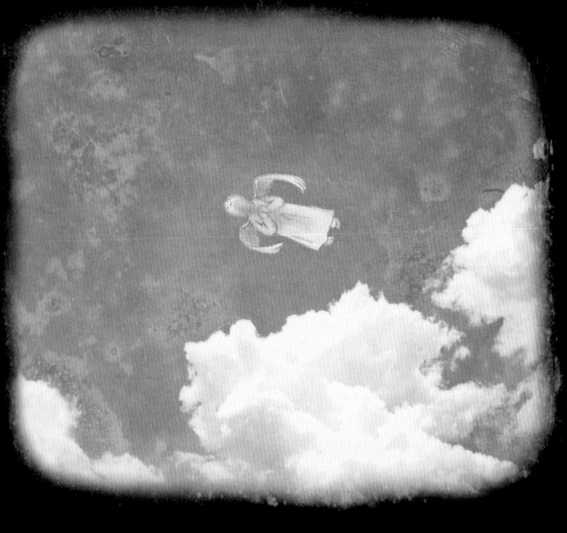

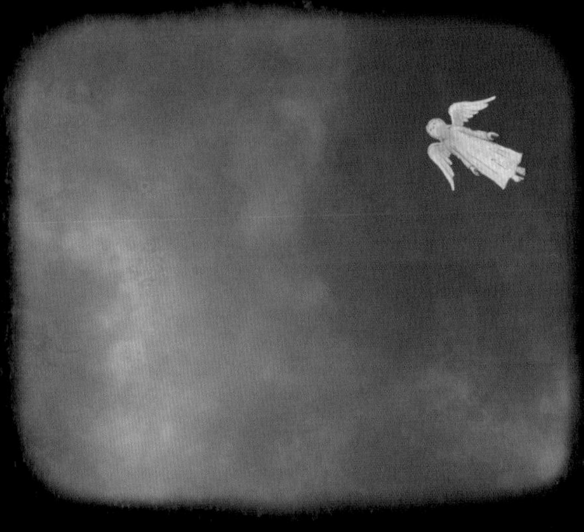

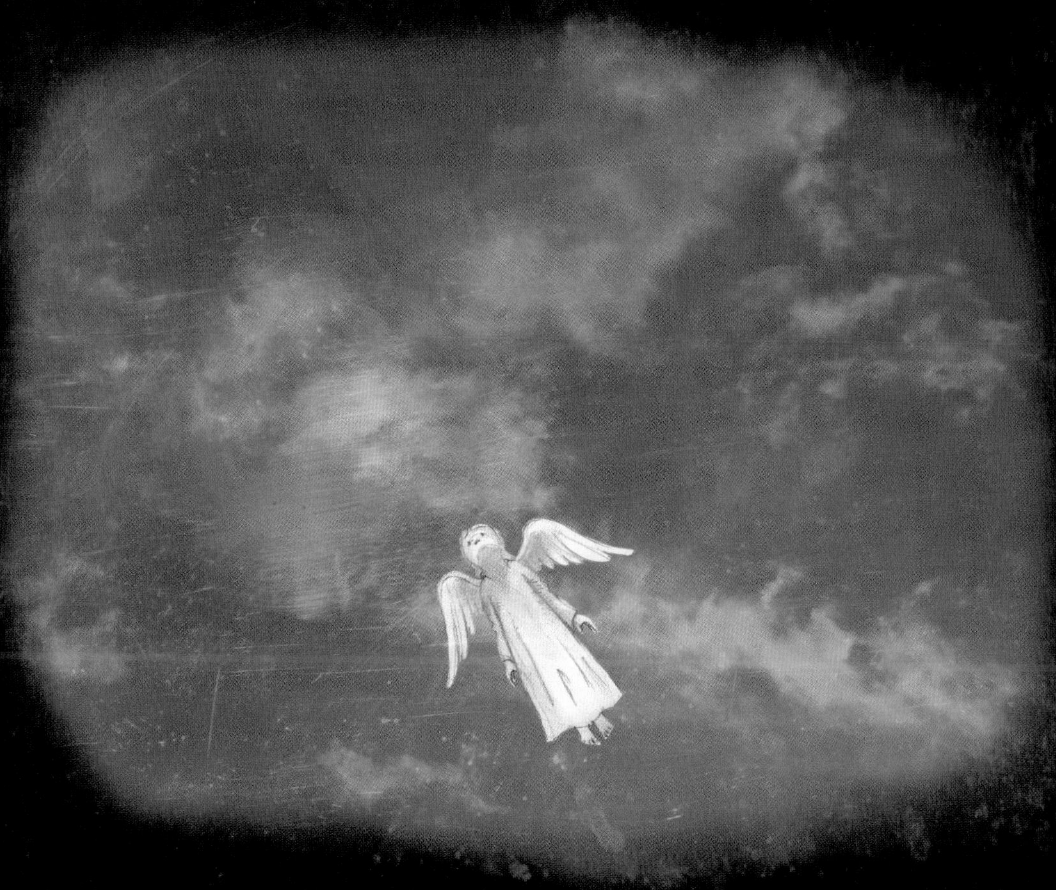

of light

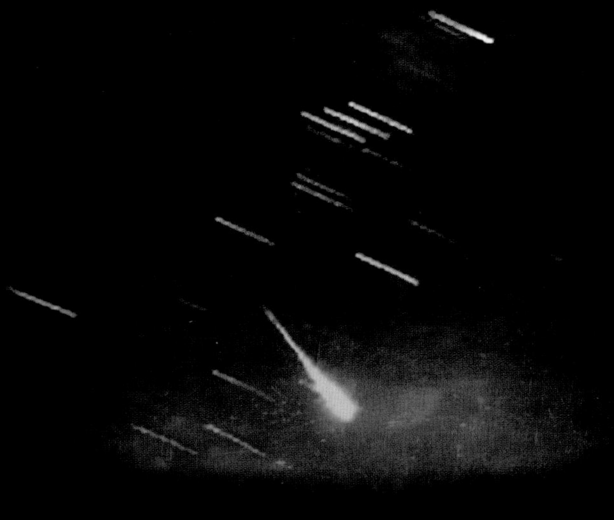

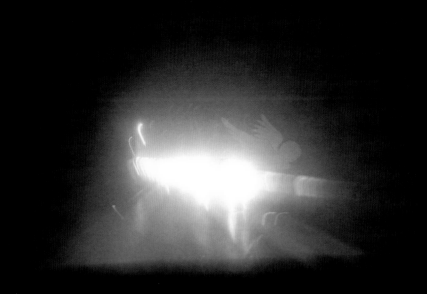

no eye is sure it's seen.

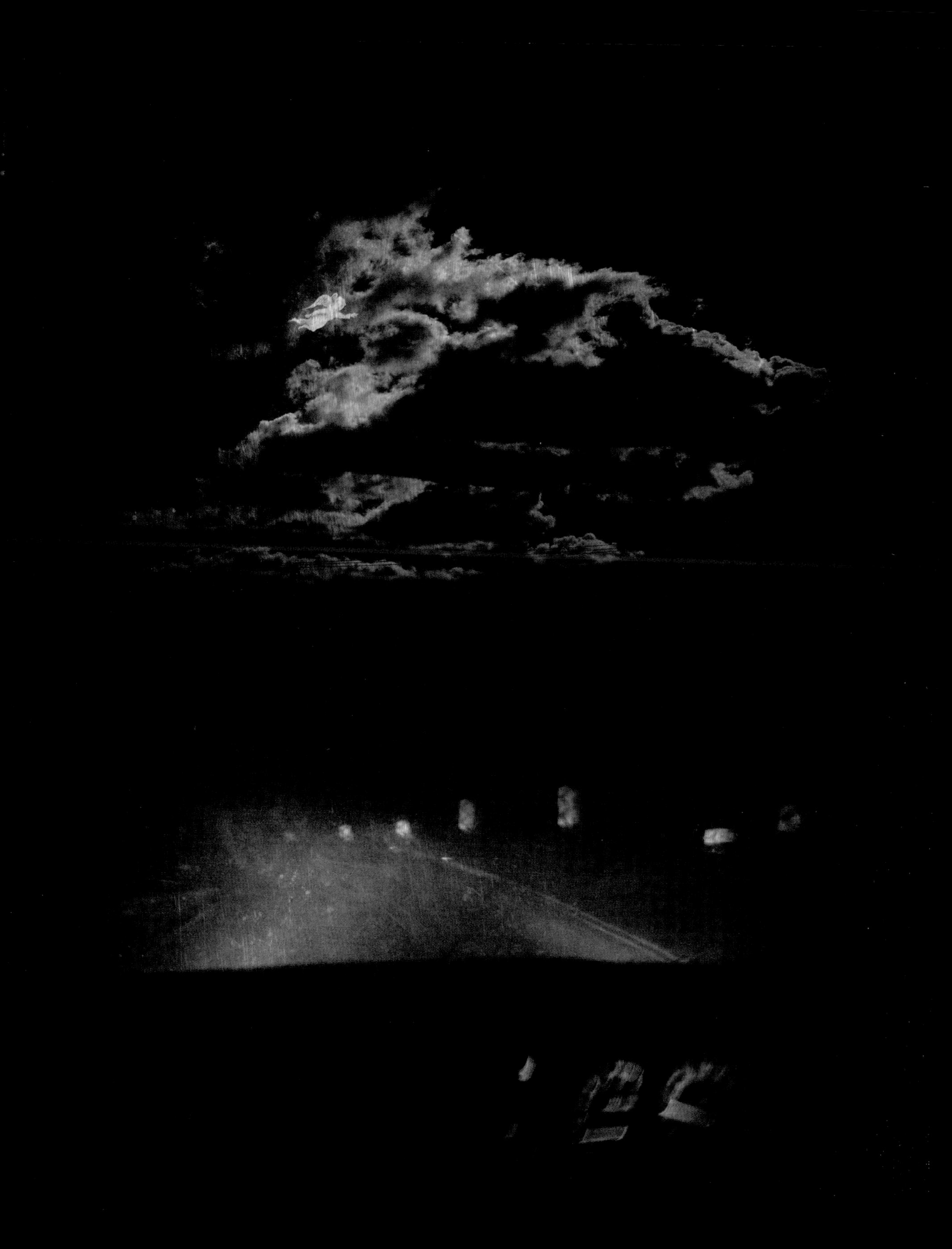

Like a thought

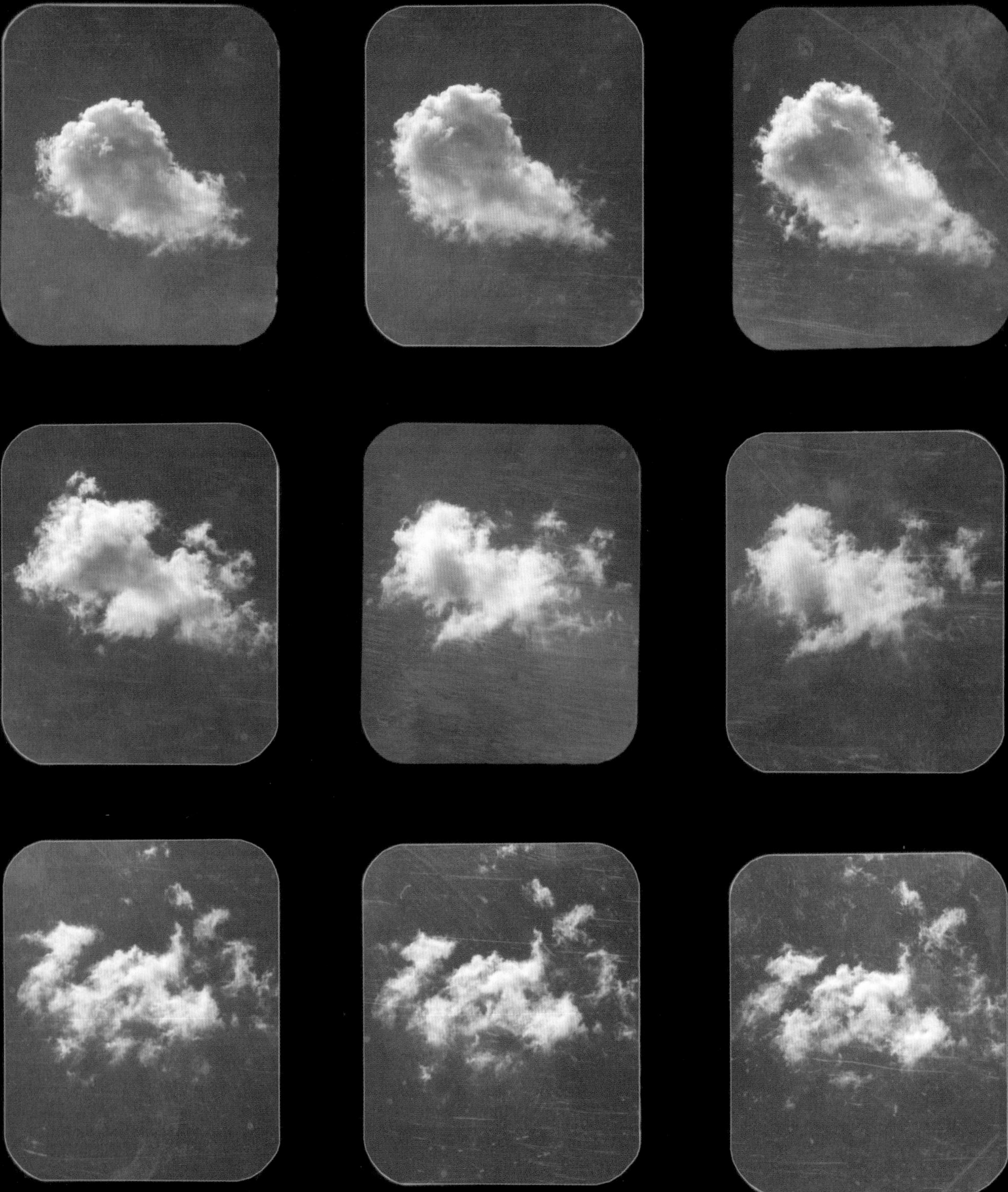

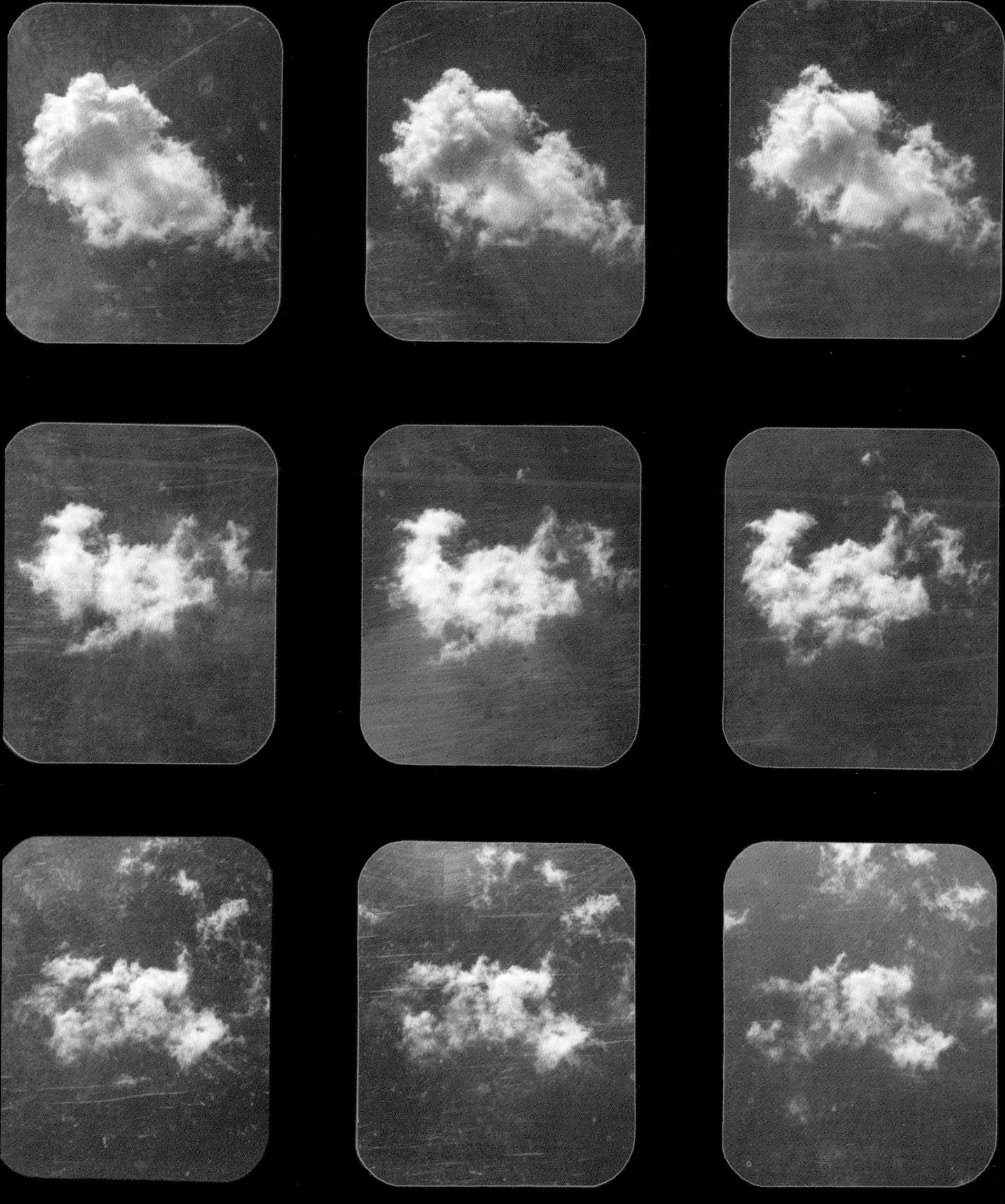

hard to hold.

They come

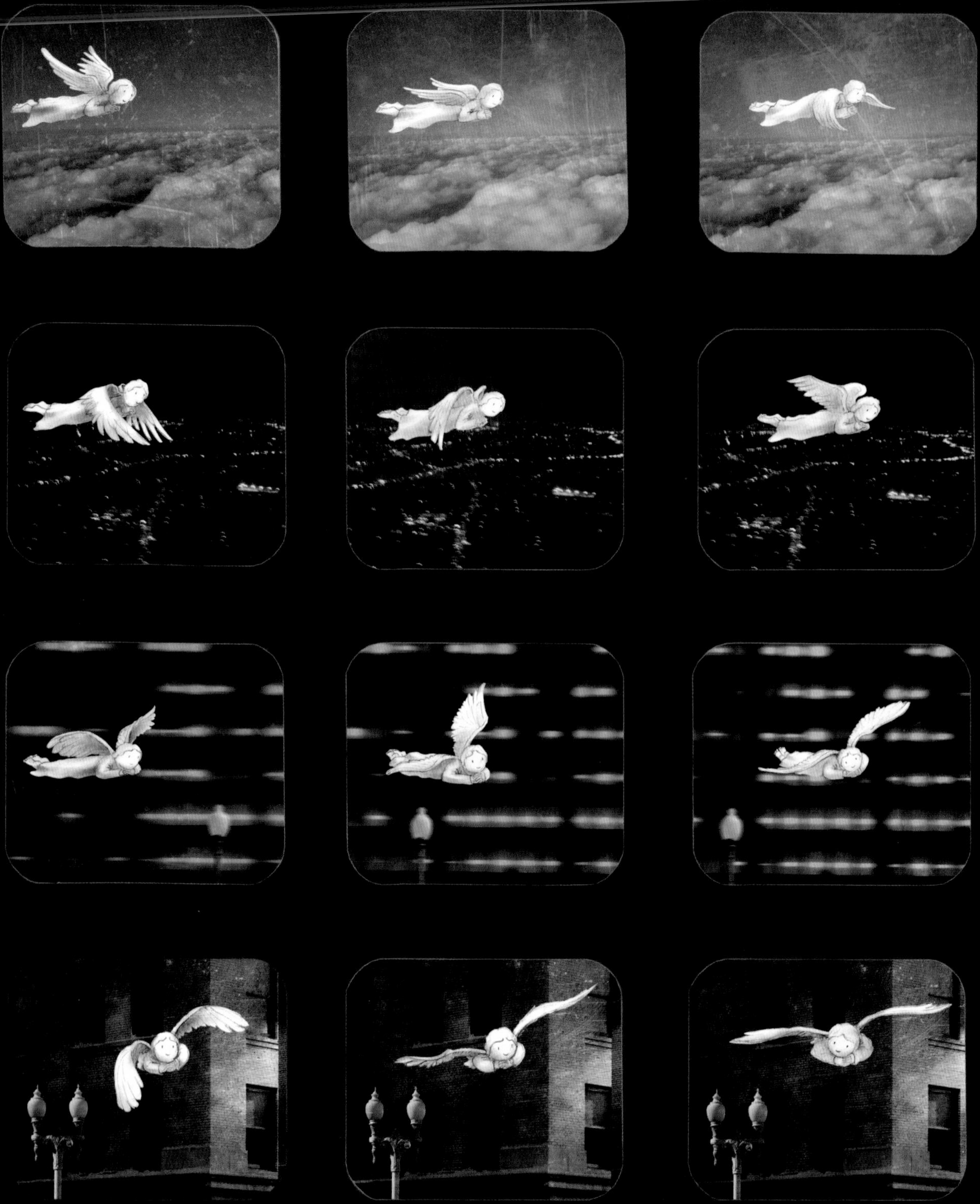

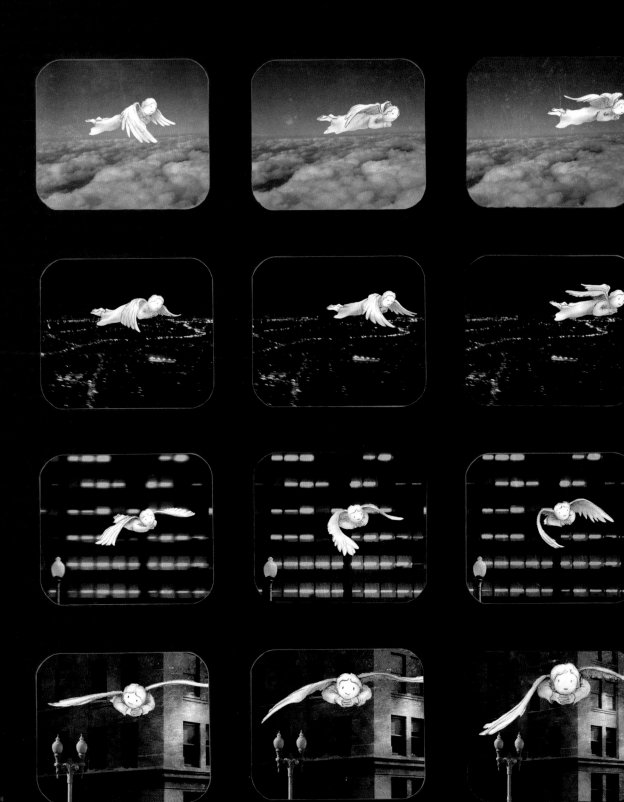

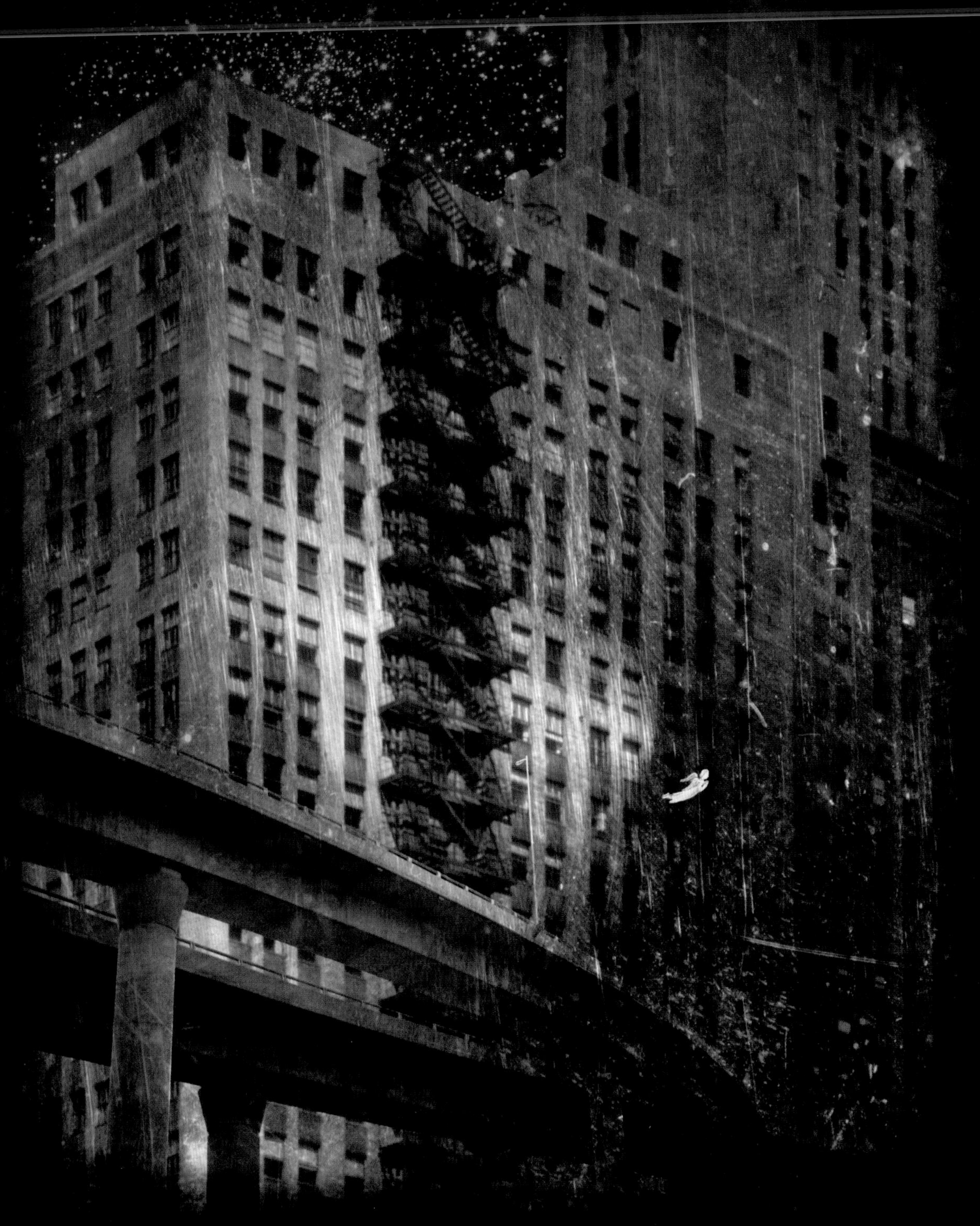

to watch over

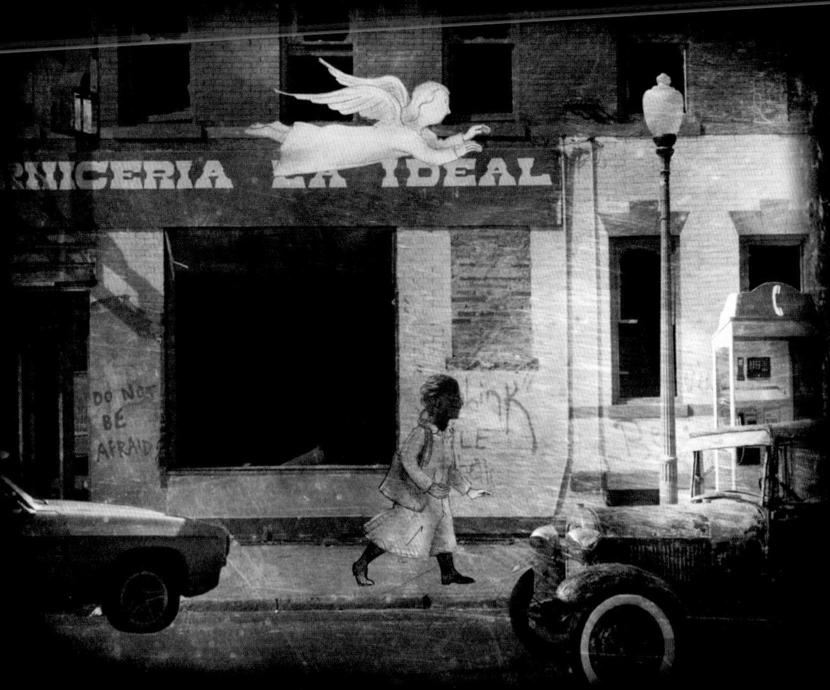
DO NOT
BE
AFRAID

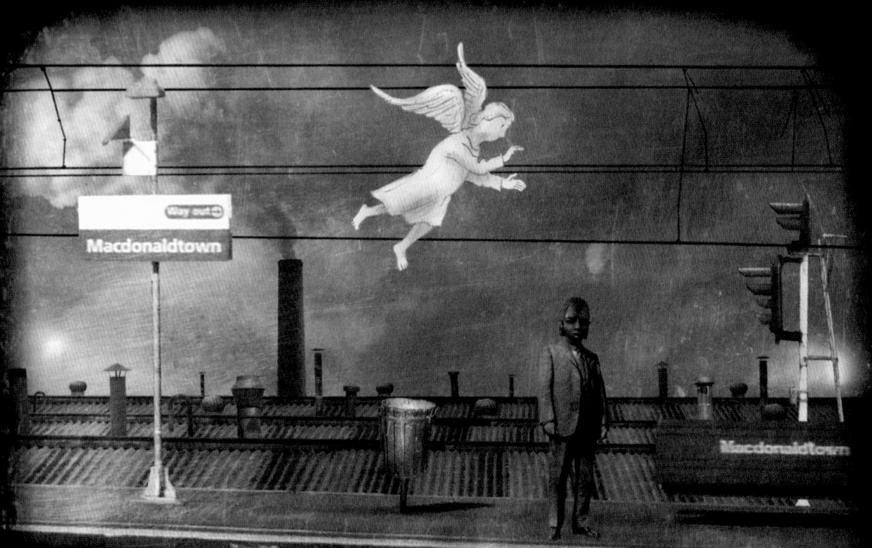
Way out
Macdonaldtown
Macdonaldtown

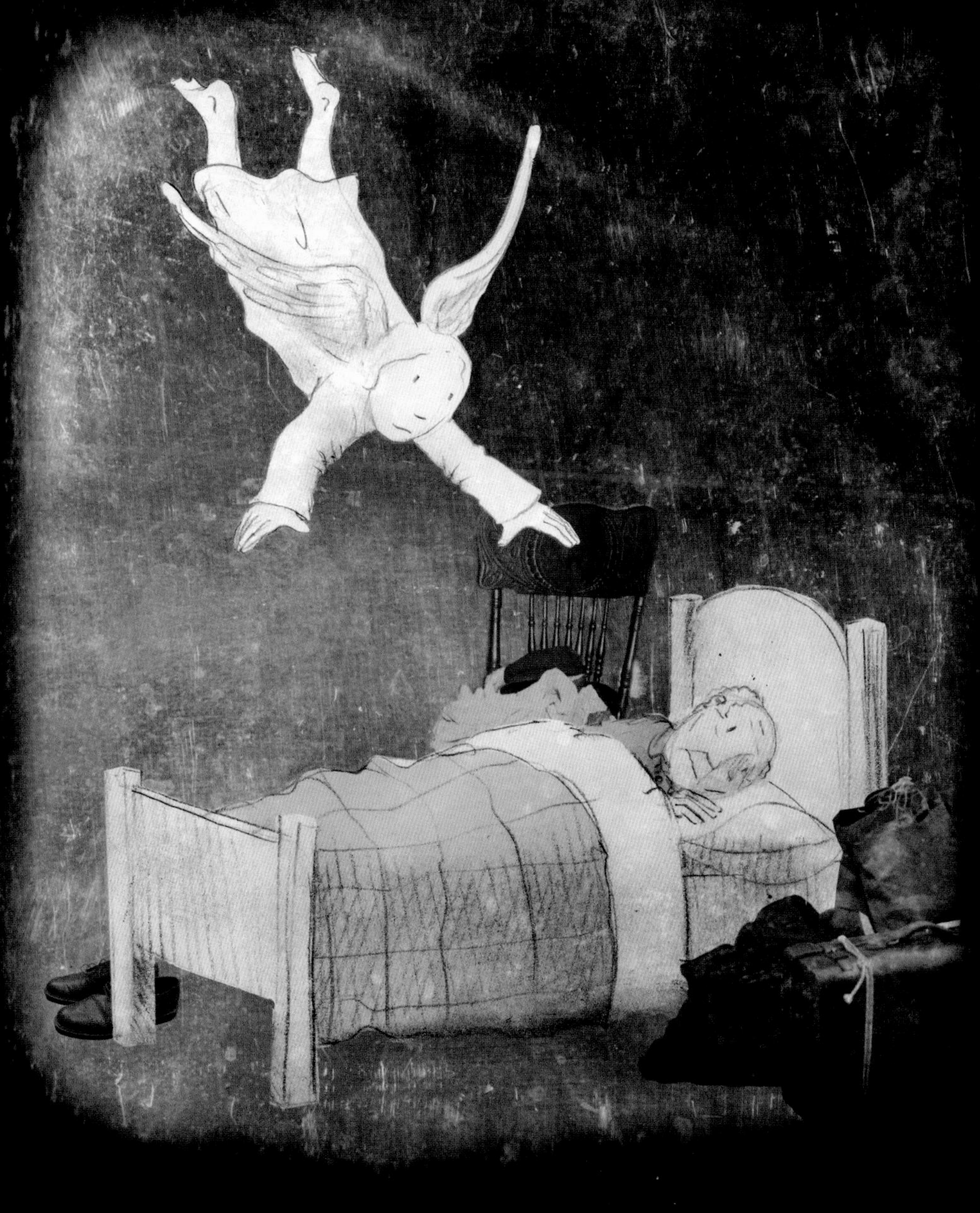

and to warm

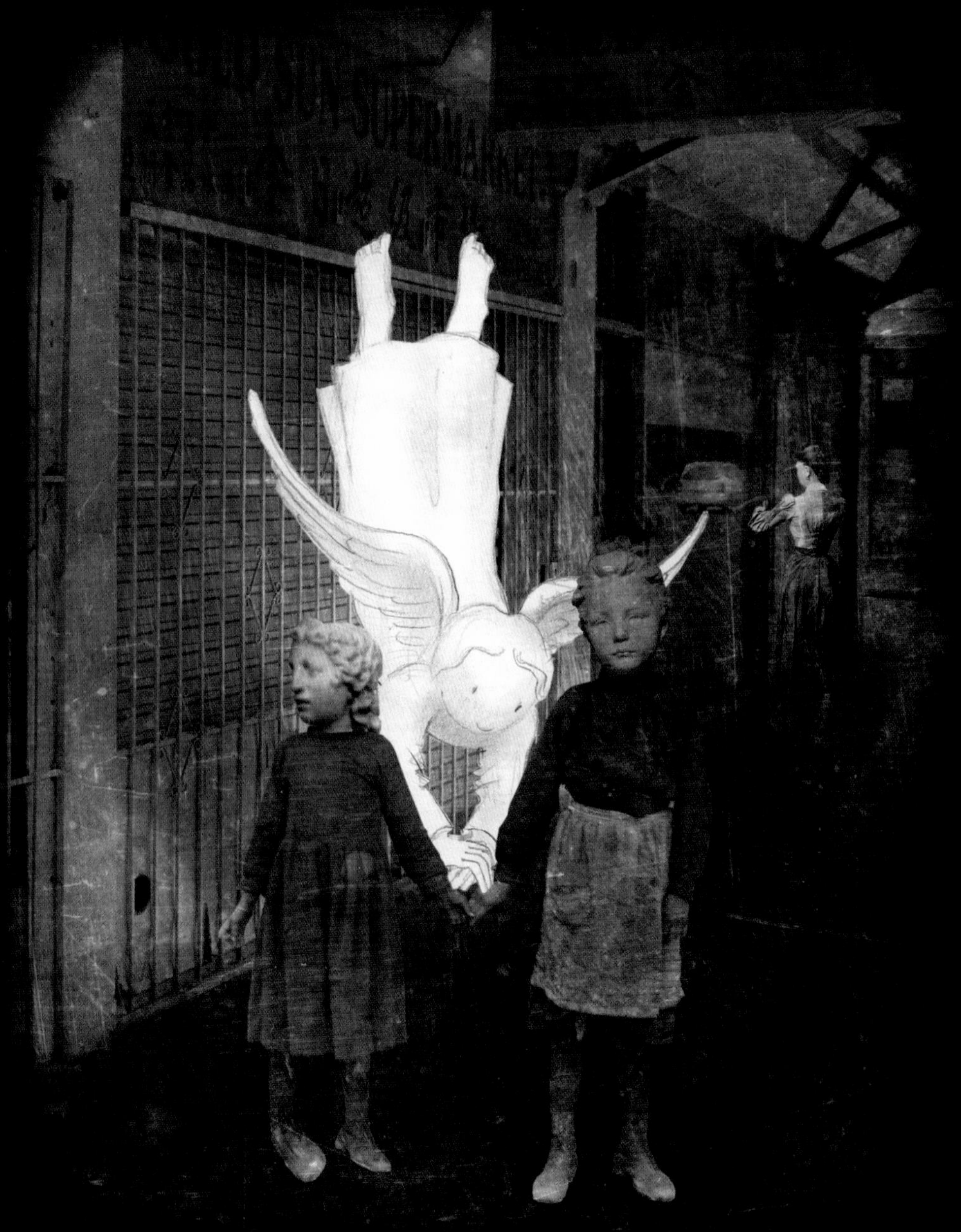

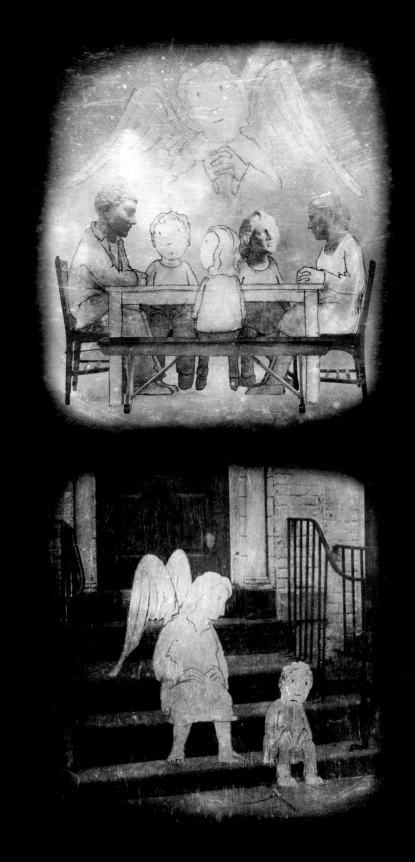

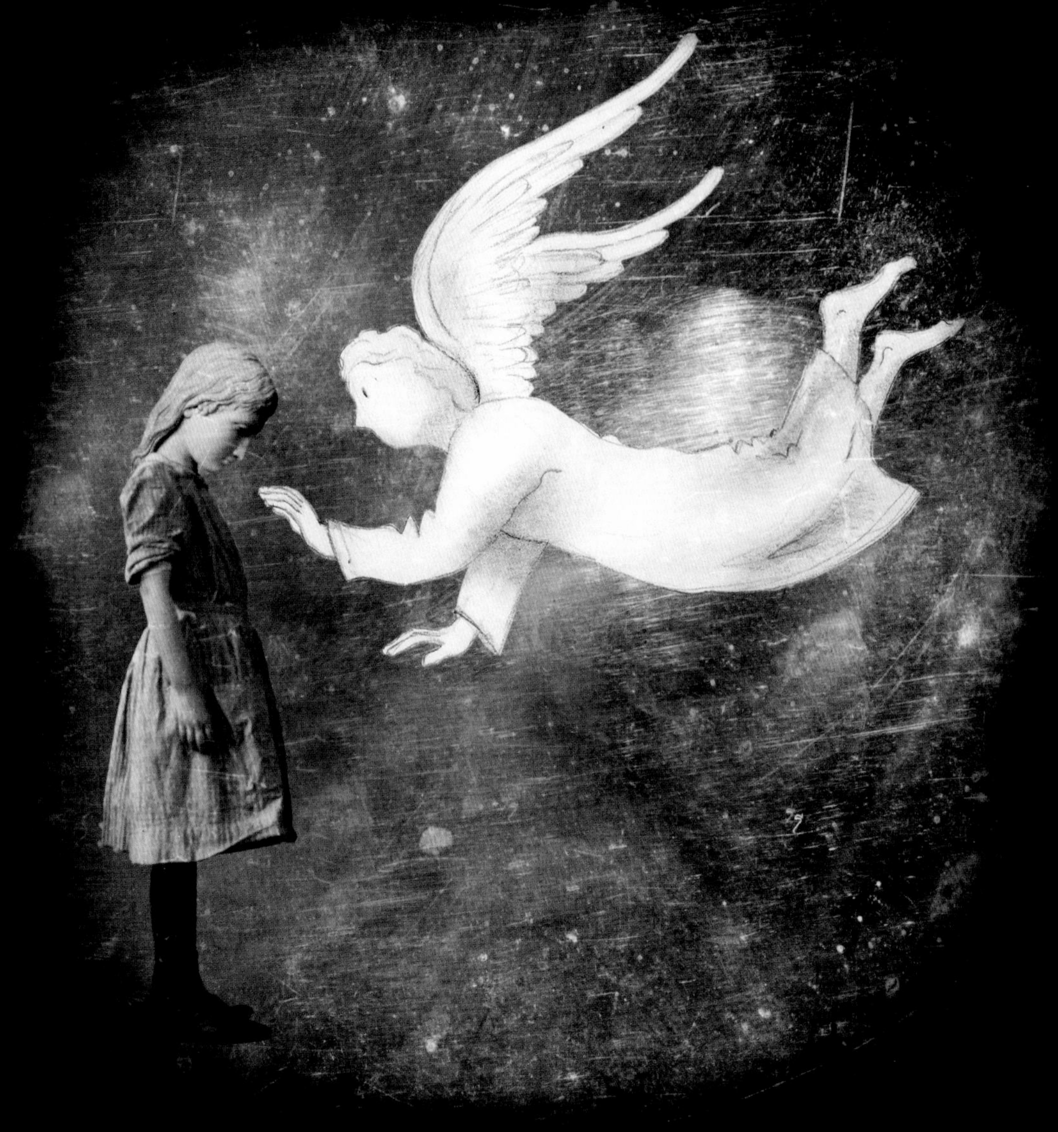

and to mend.

II

But their work is not easy

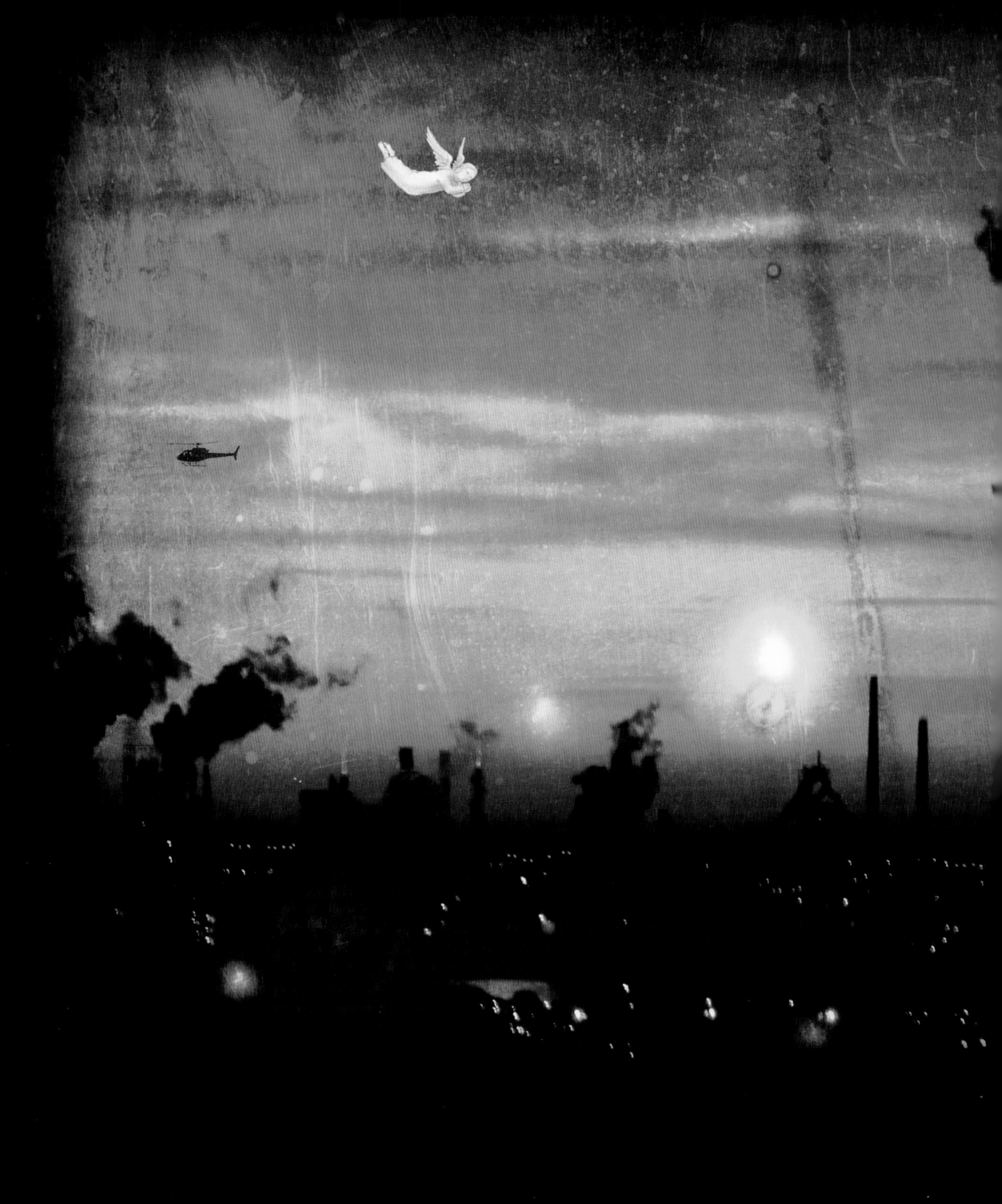

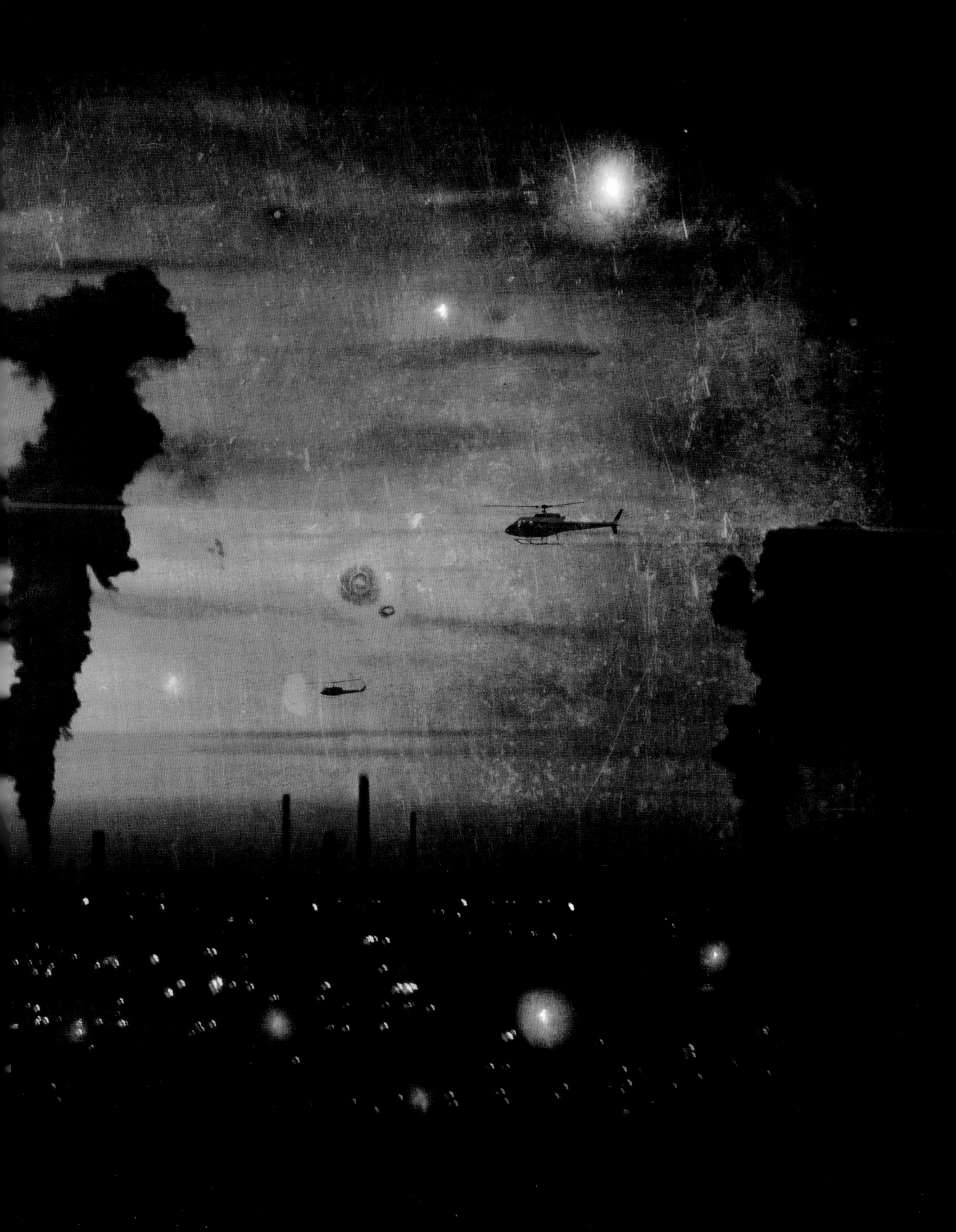

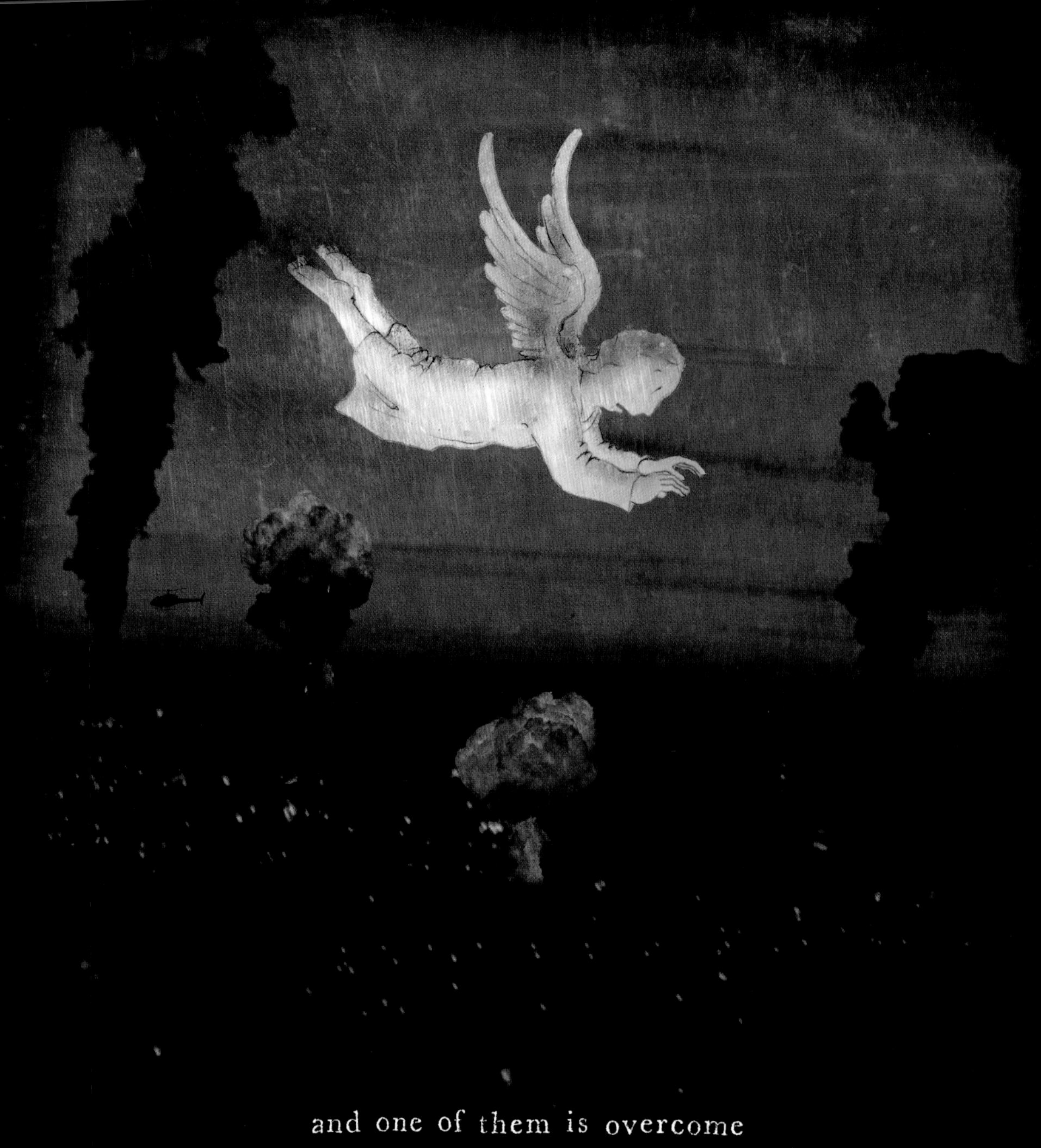

and one of them is overcome

and sinks

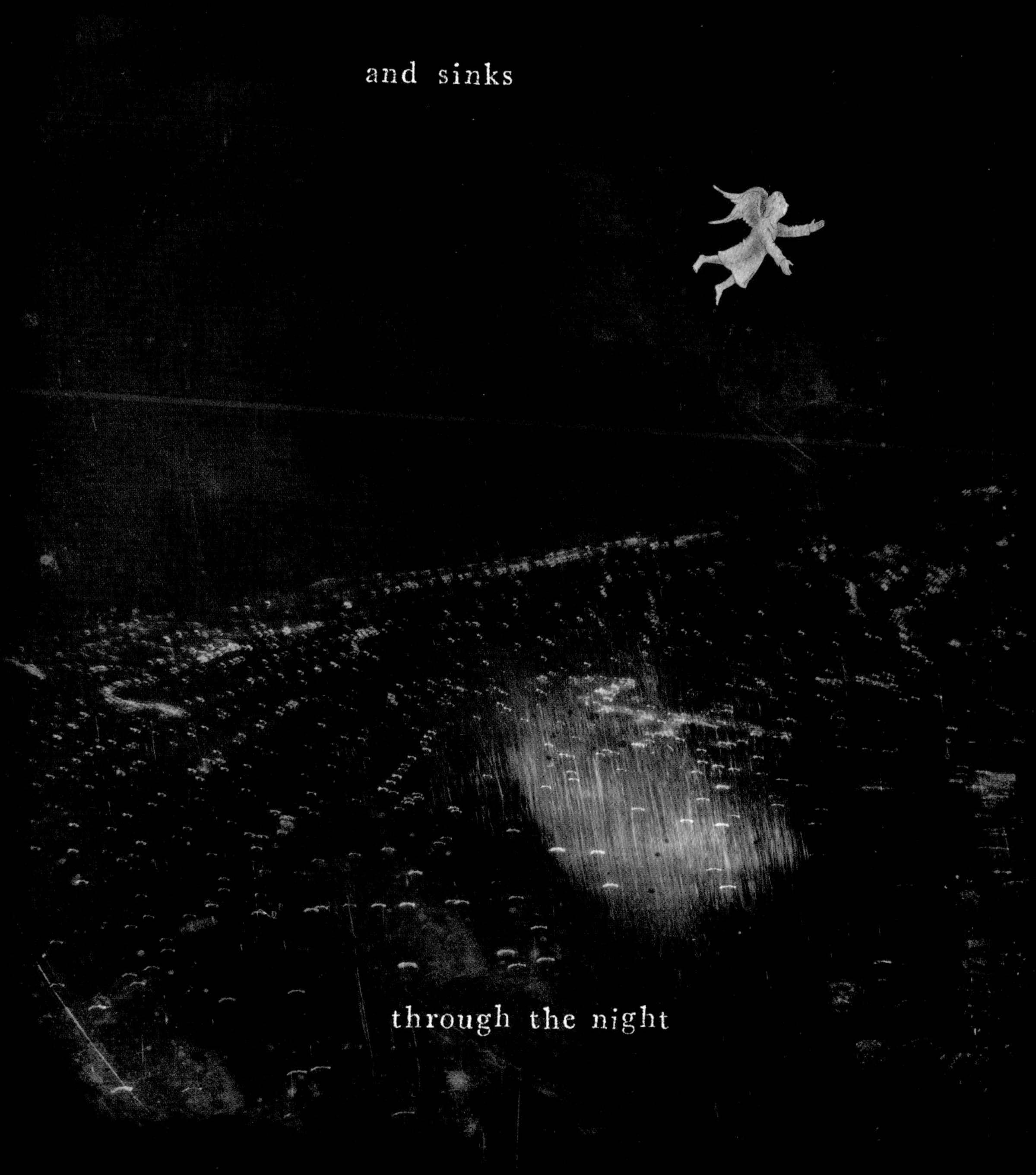

through the night

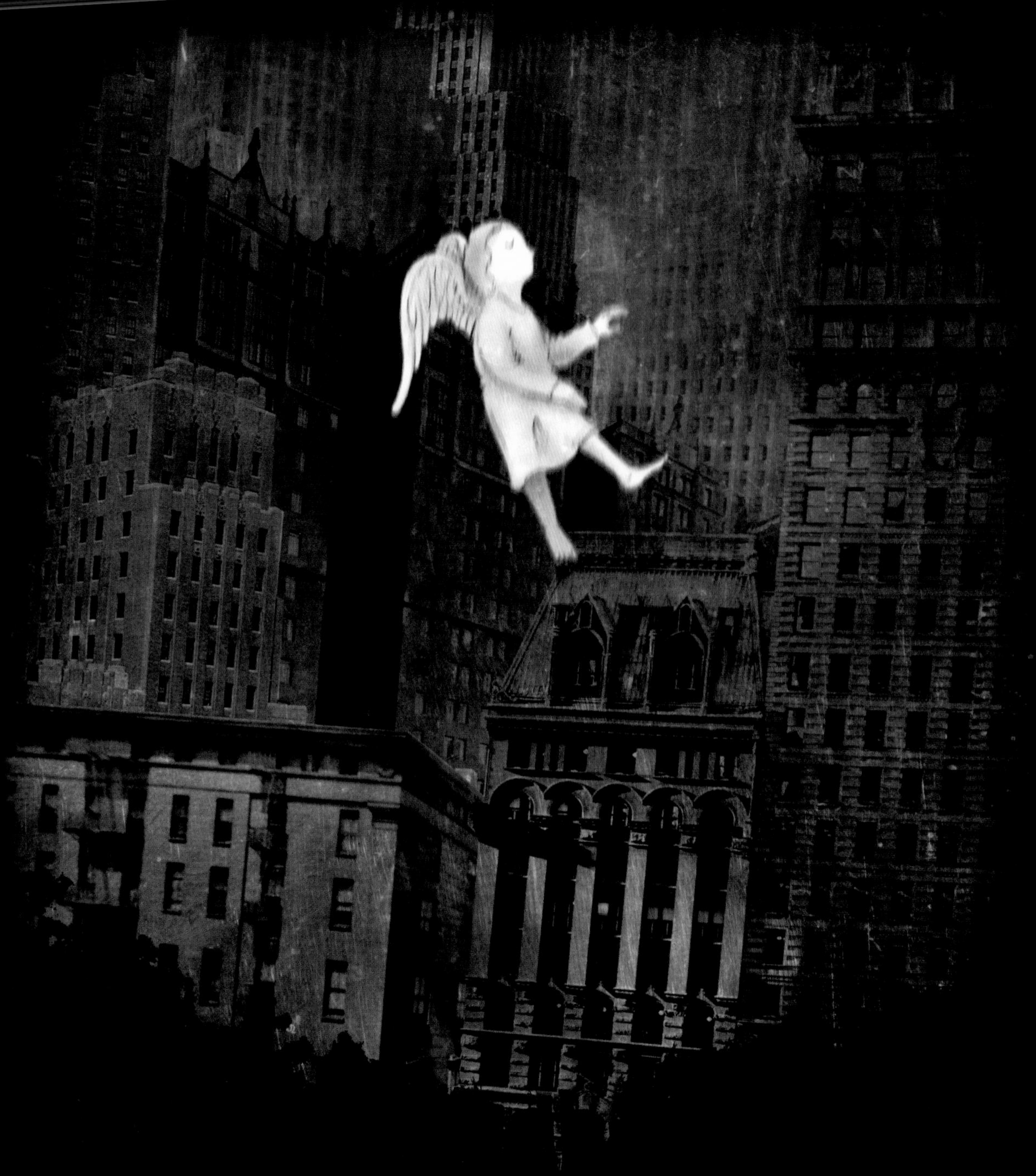

to ground.

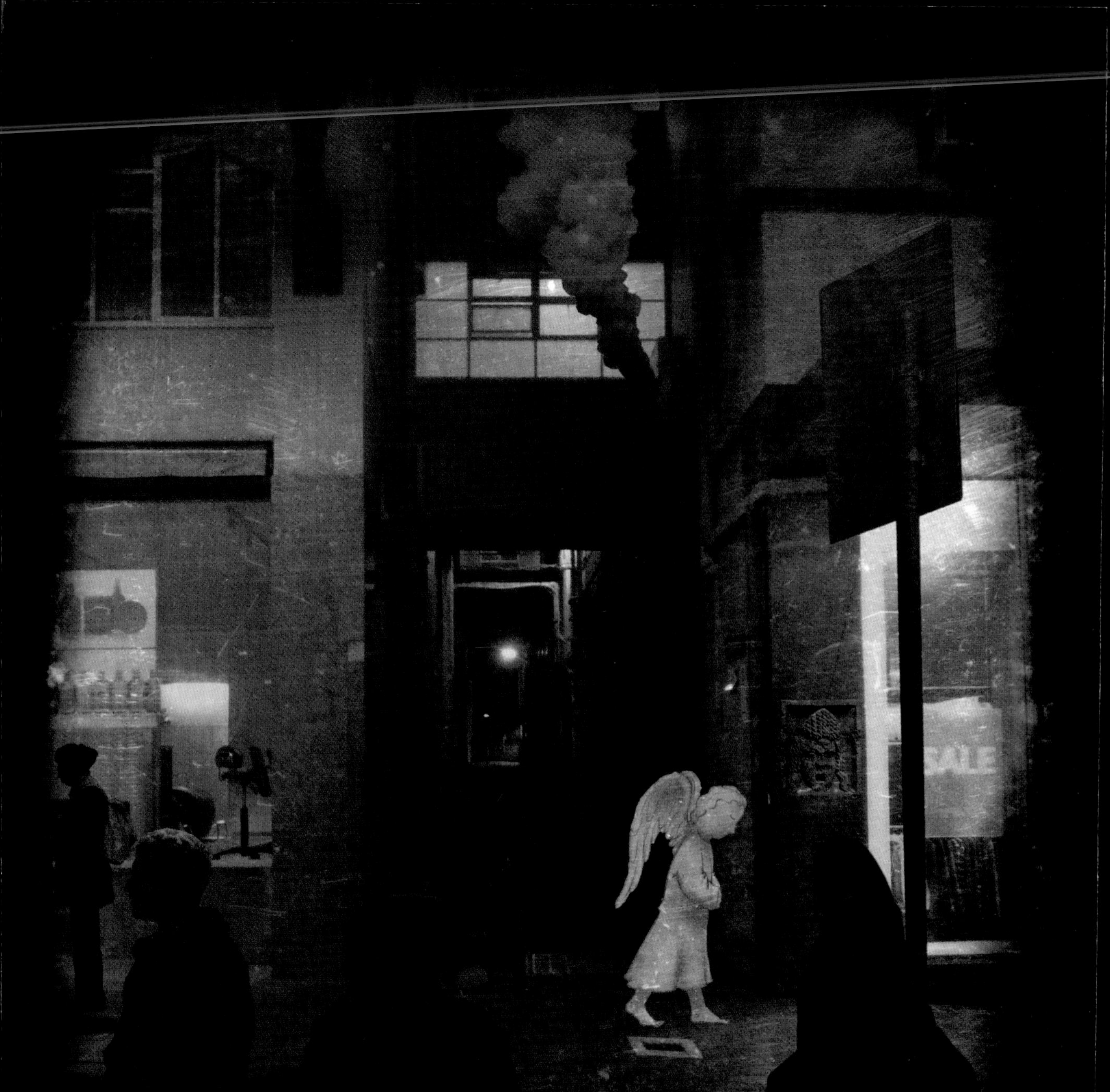
SALE

Weakened, it wanders

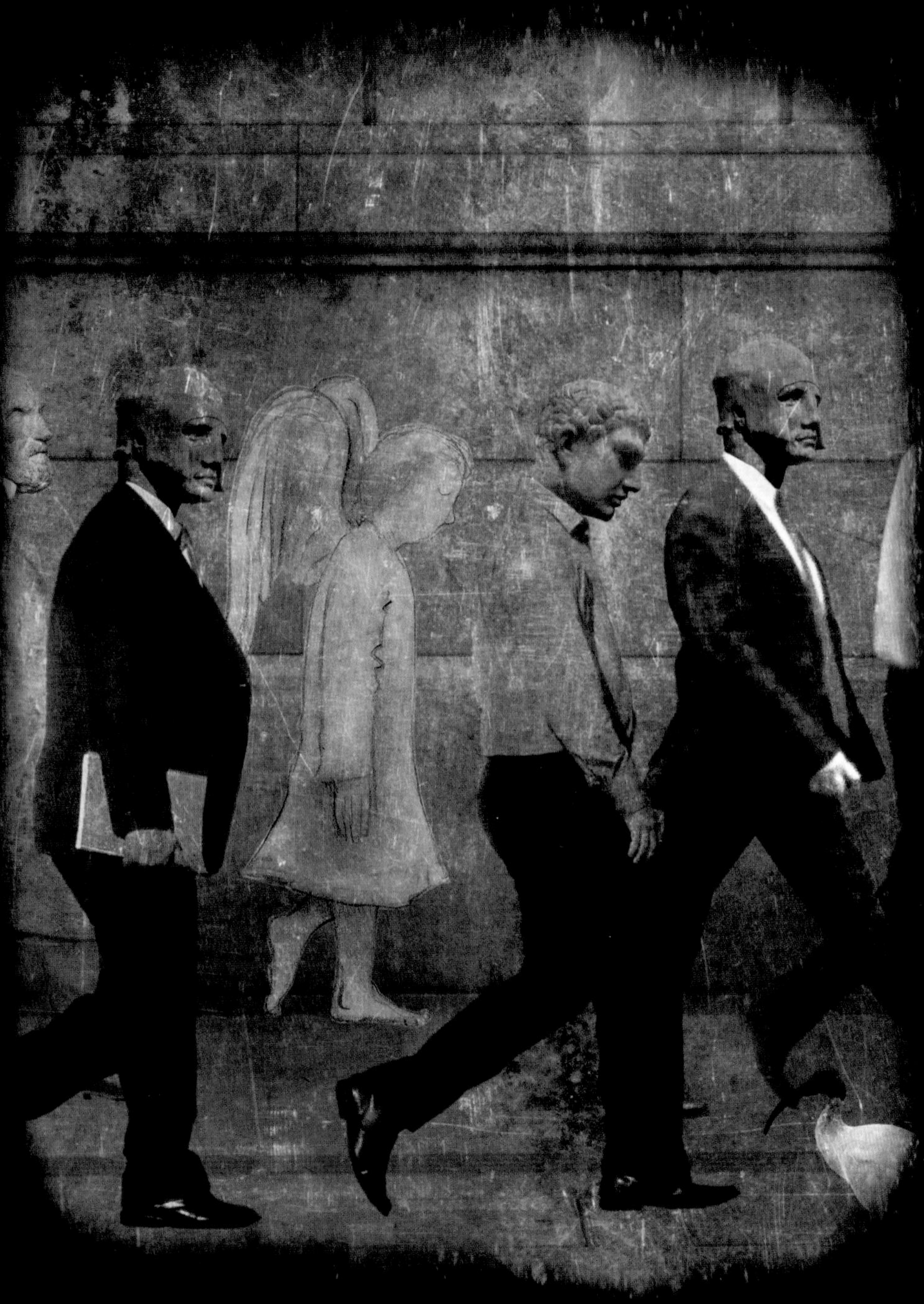

as if dreaming

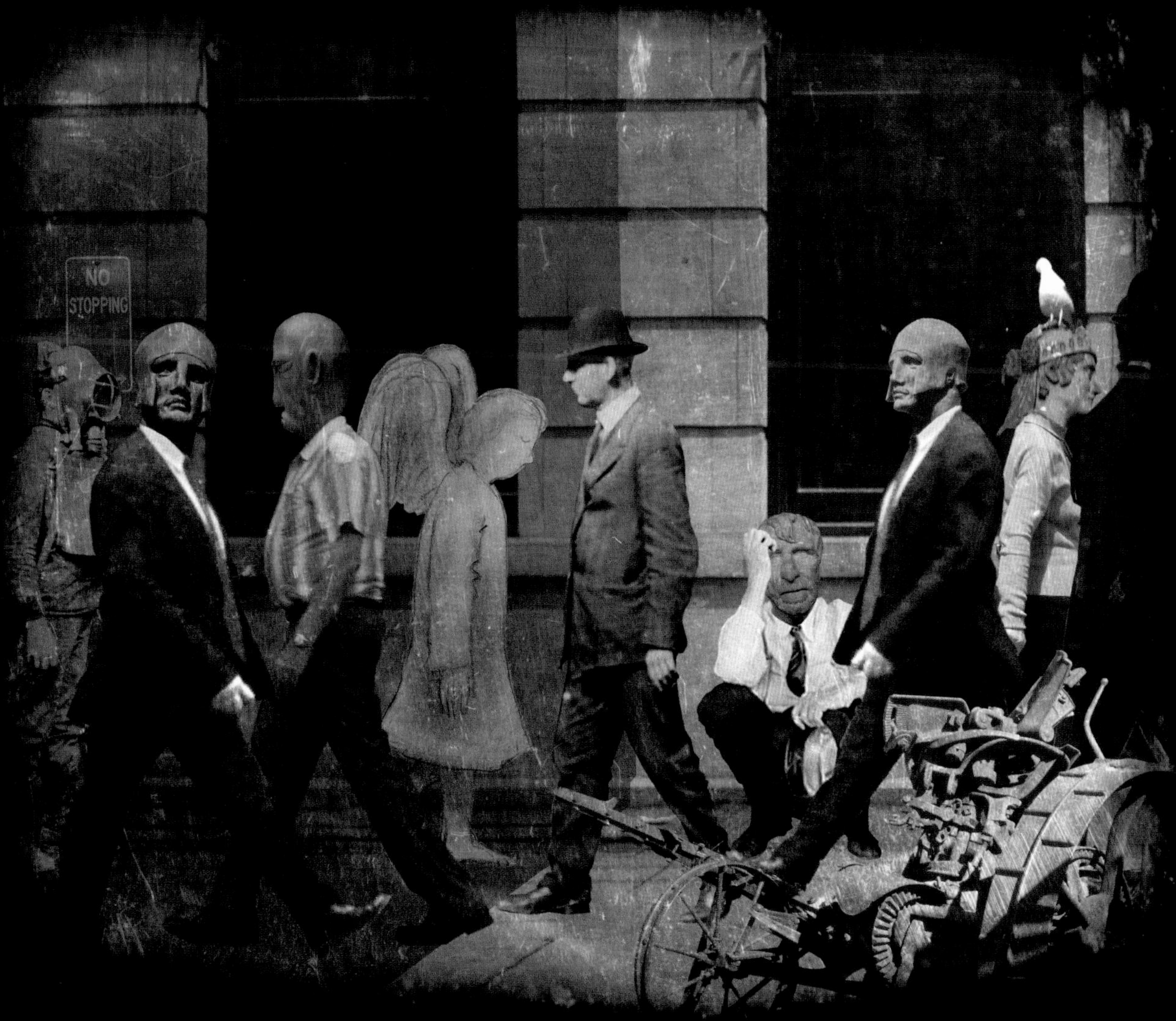
NO
STOPPING

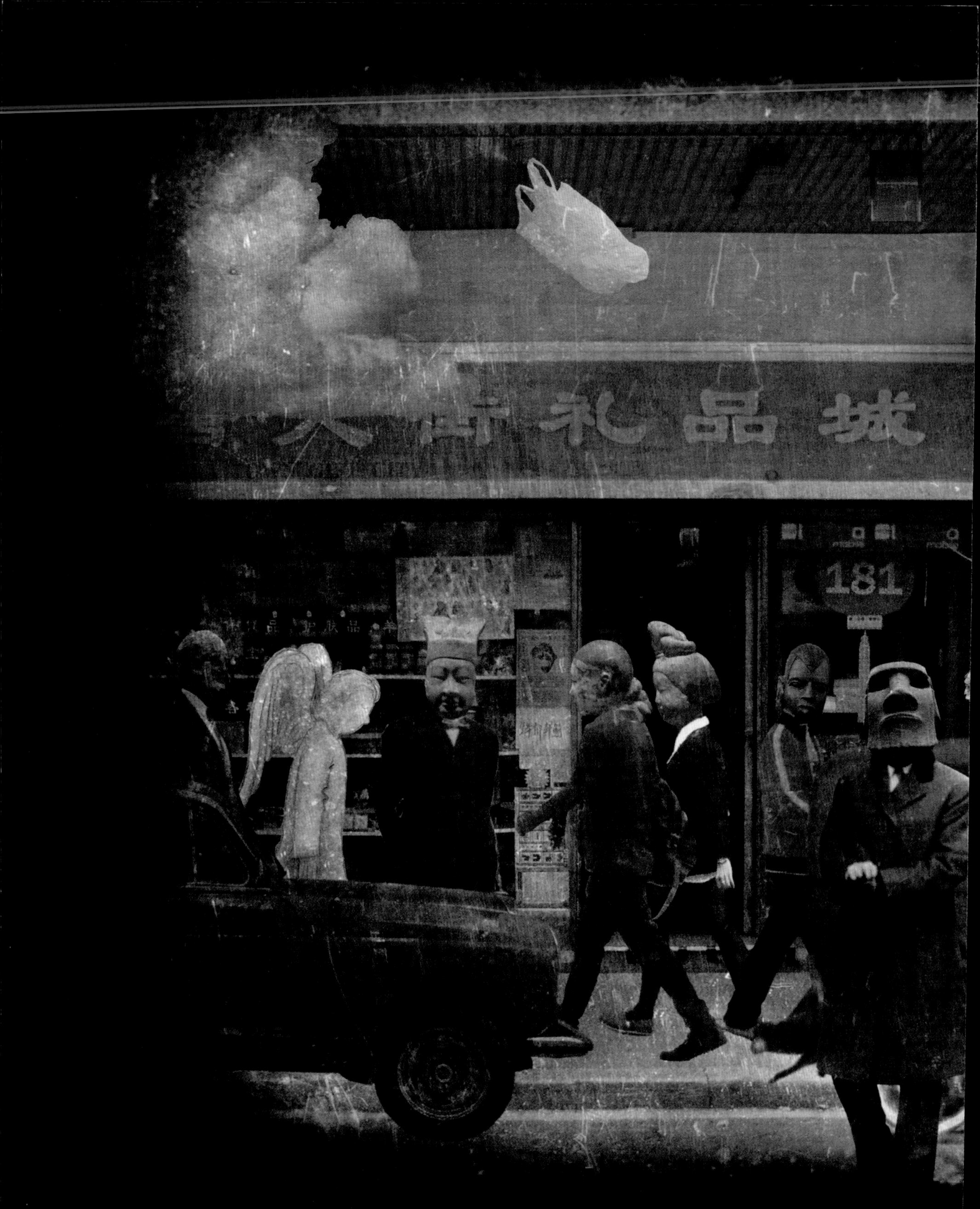

礼品城
181

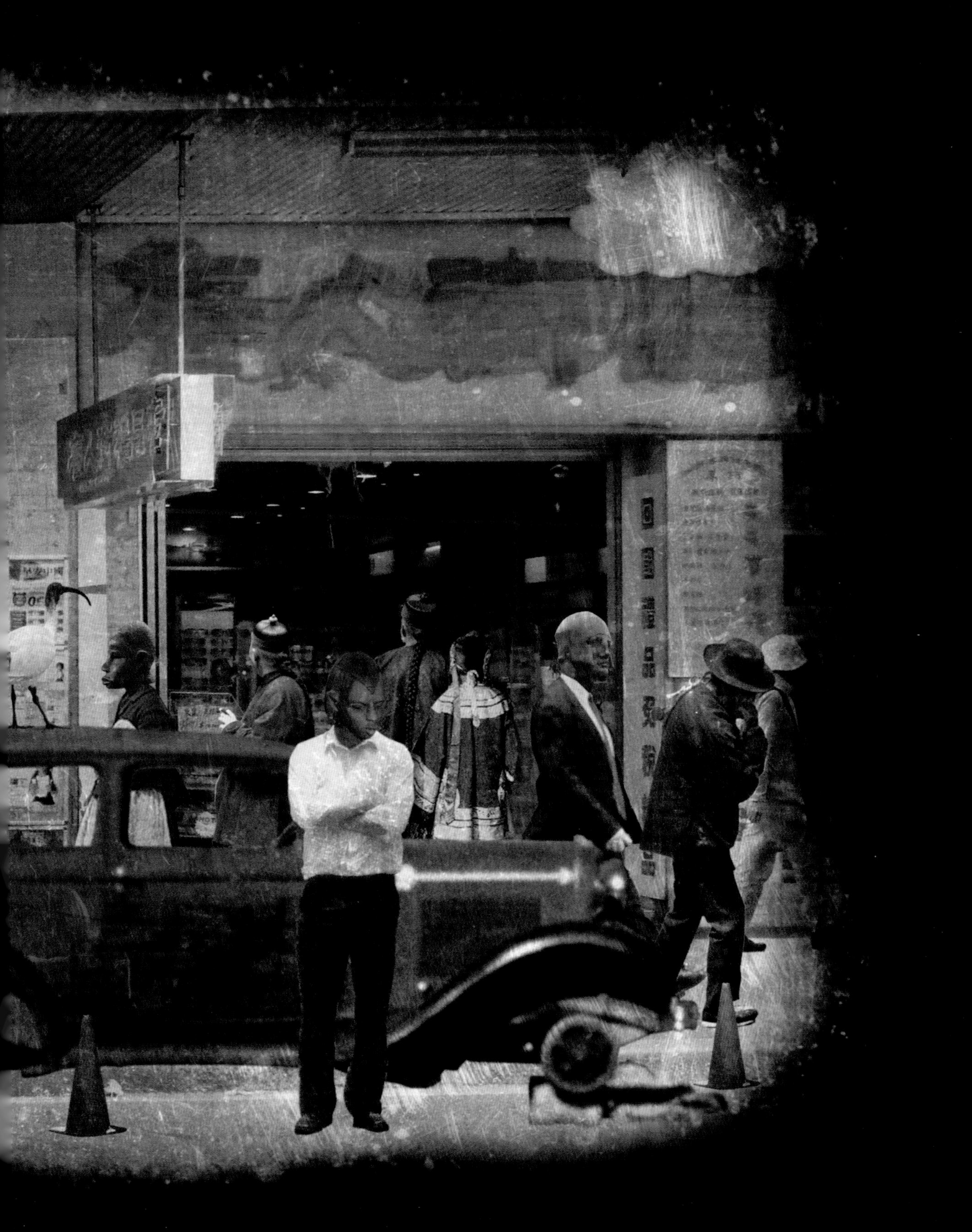

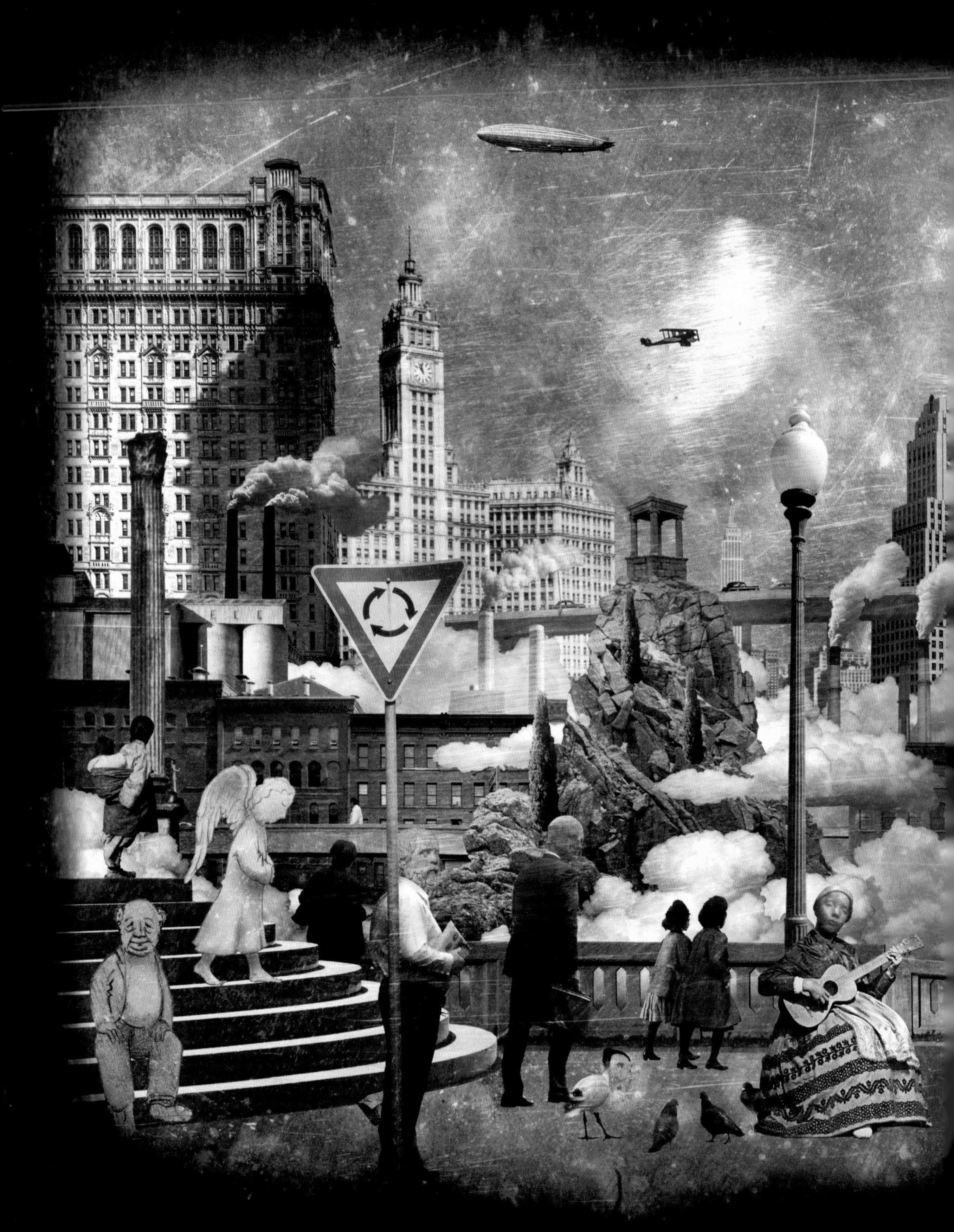

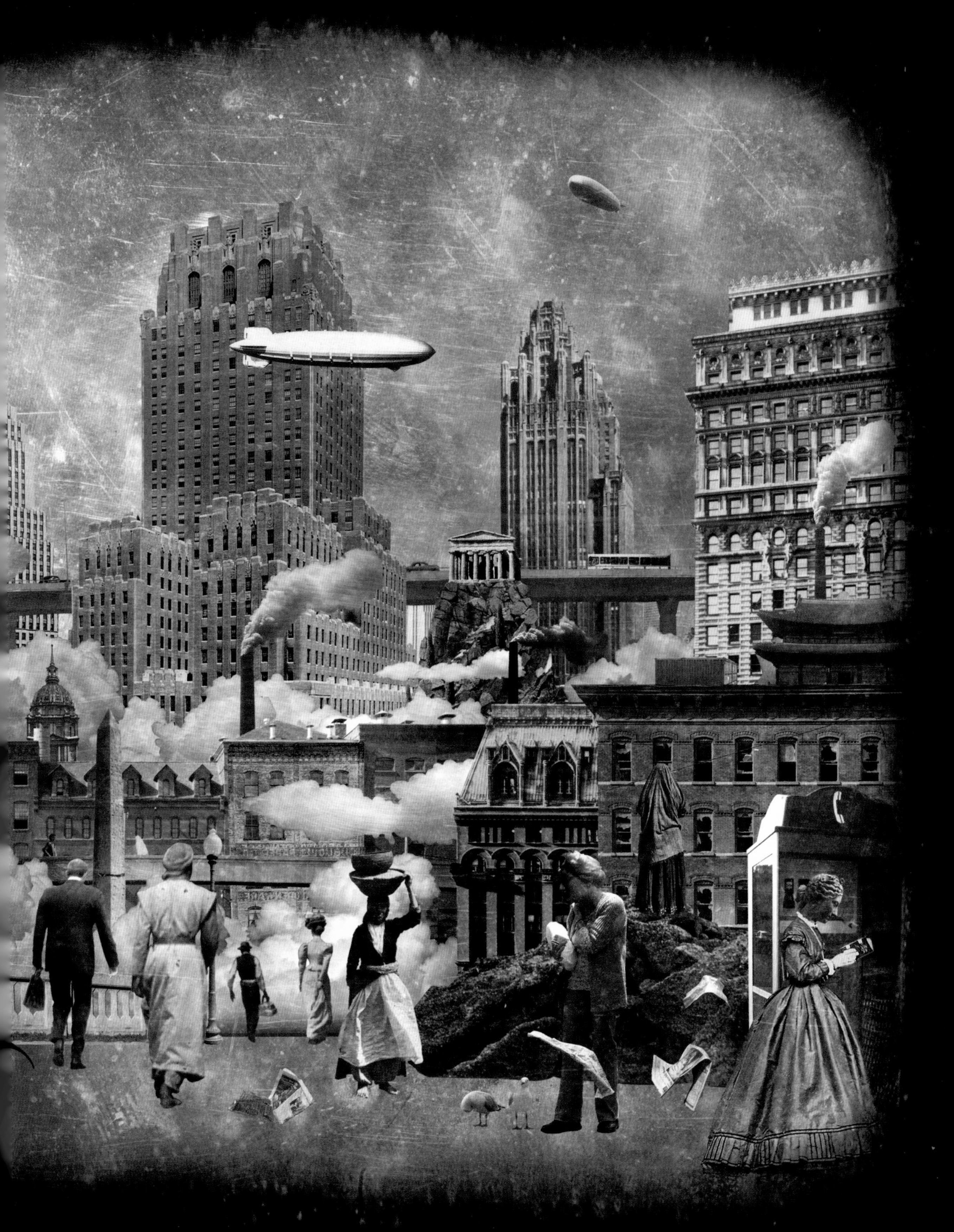

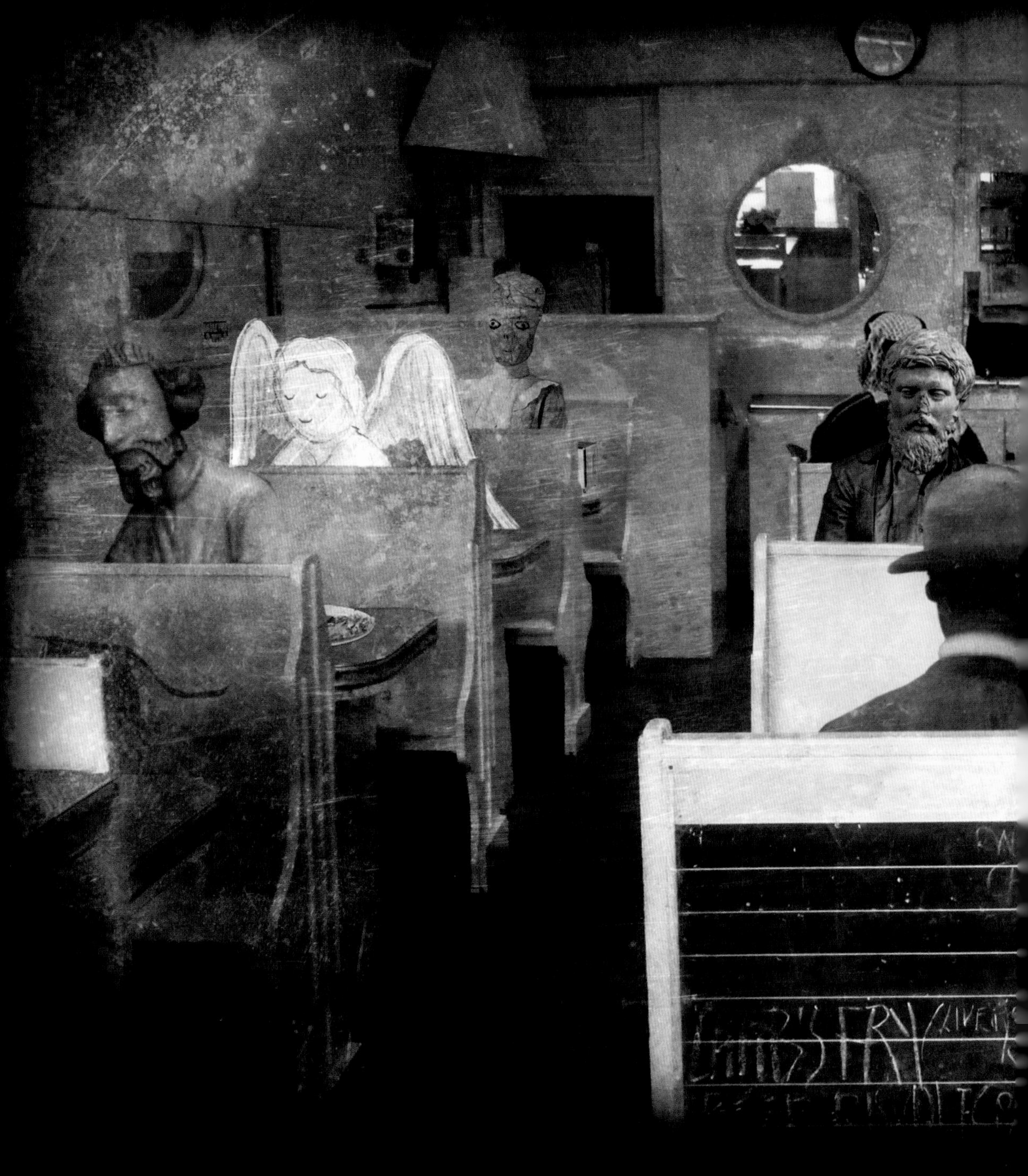

resting where it can

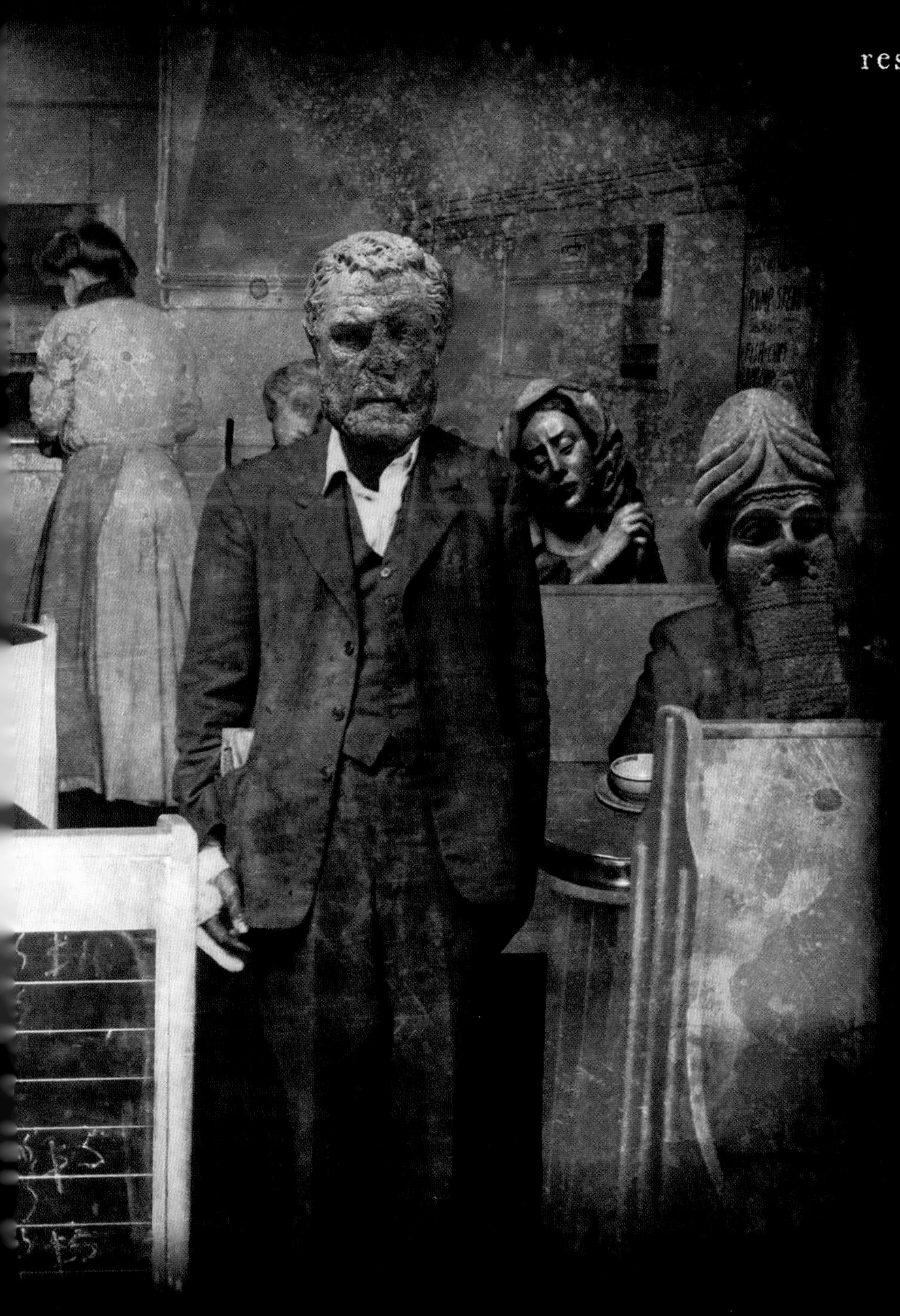

until rest is not enough

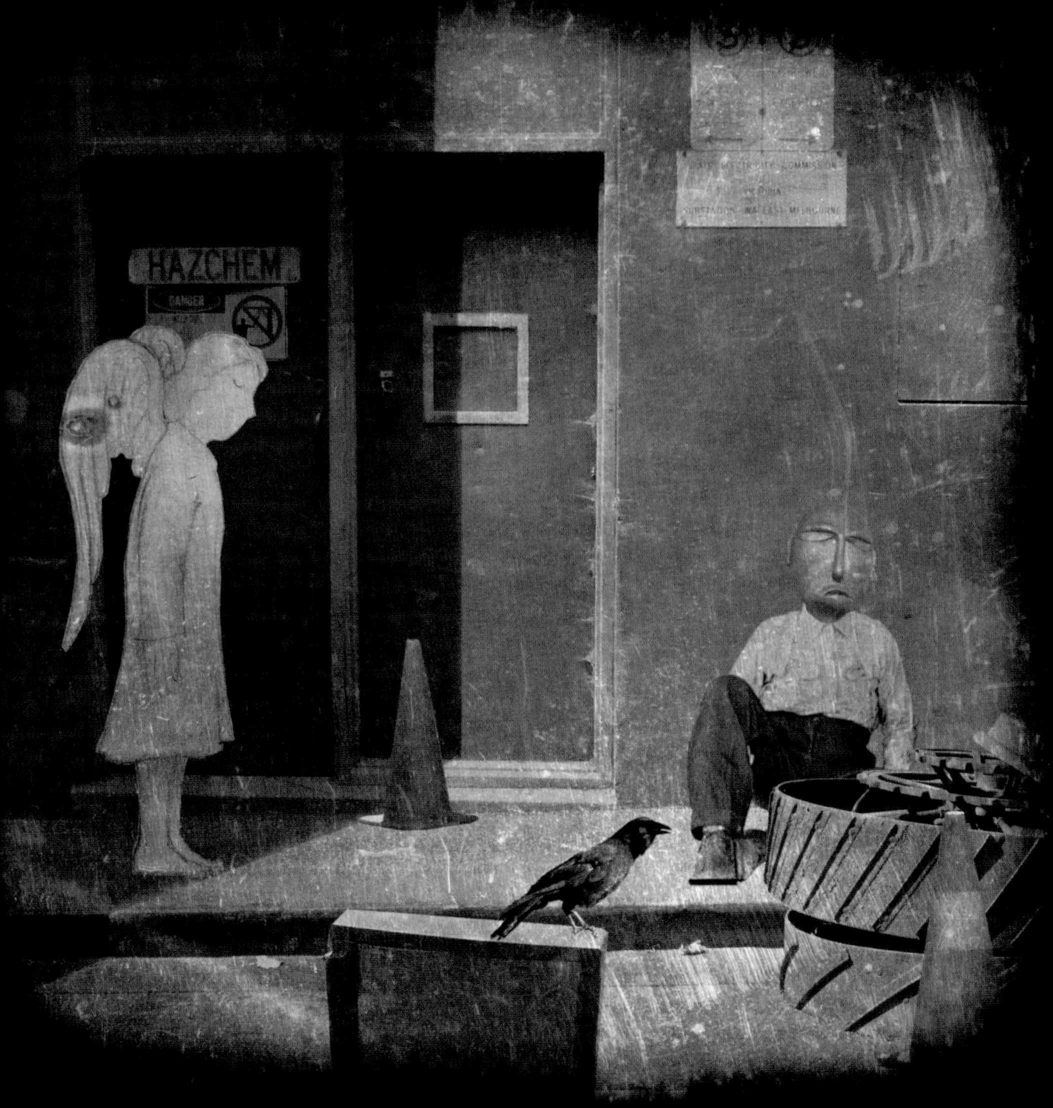
HAZCHEM

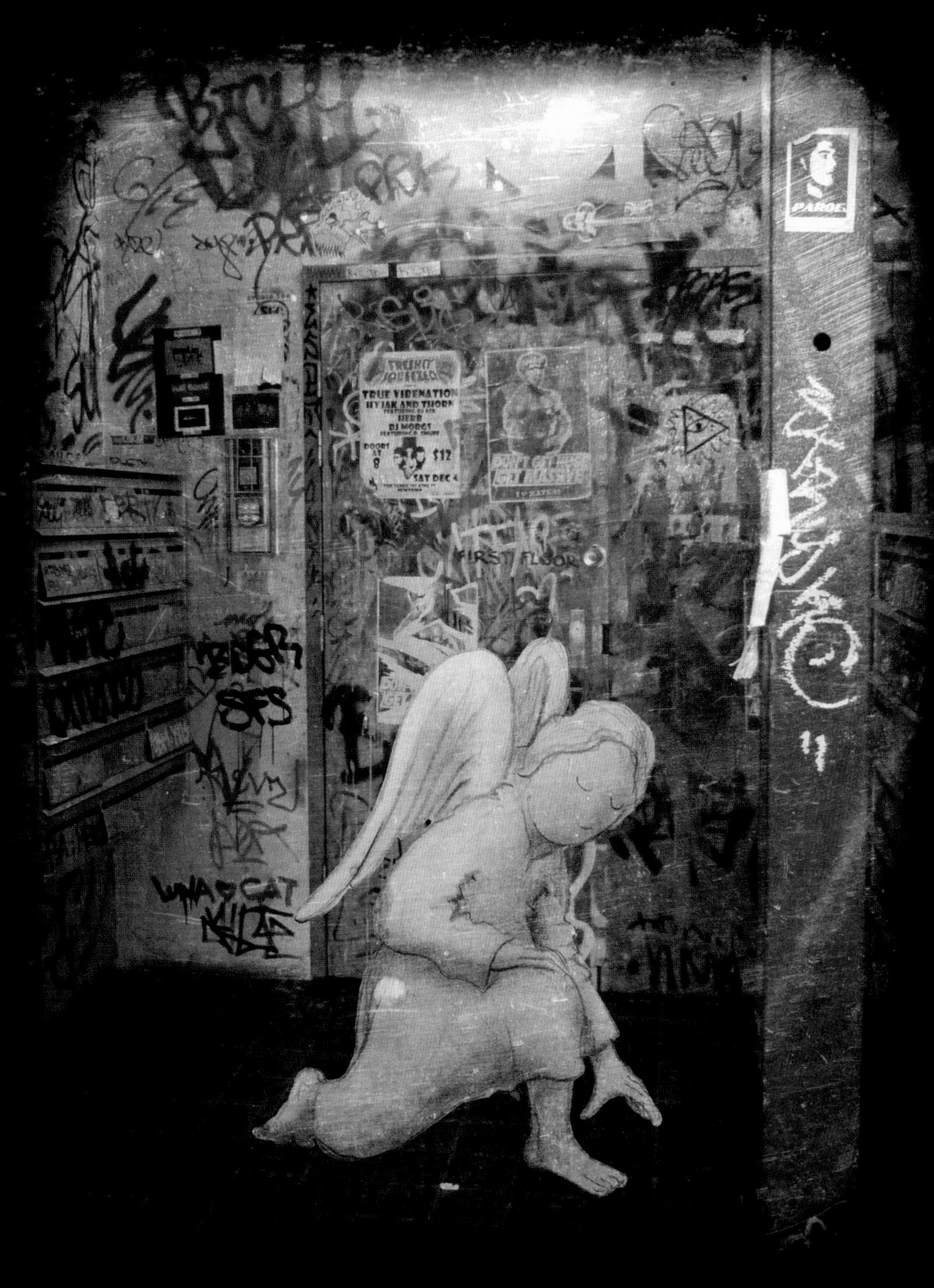

TRUE VIBENATION
DJ MORGS
$12
SAT DEC 4
FIRST FLOOR

and it comes to a stop.

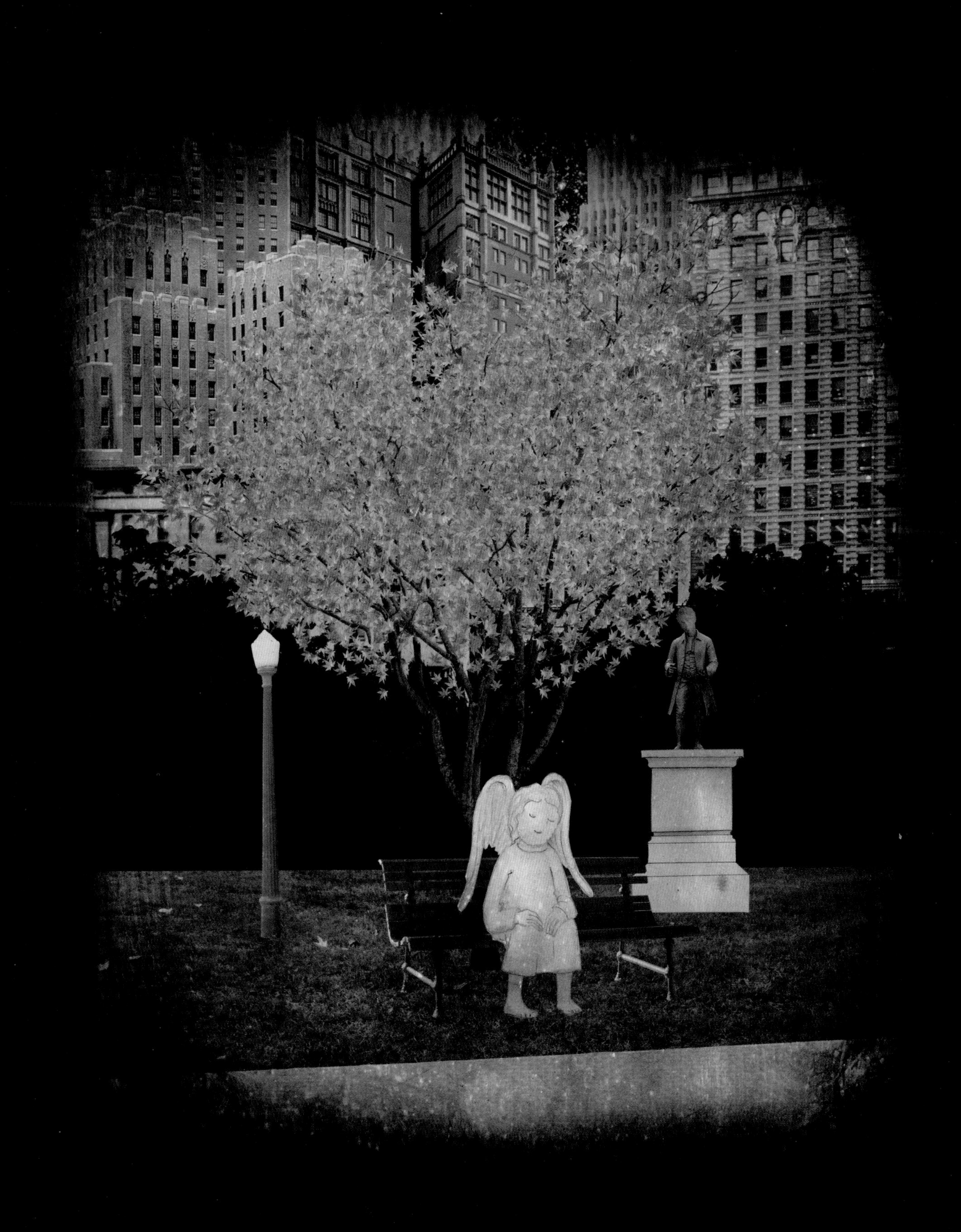

There it stays

invisible to some

growing numb and stony still

until

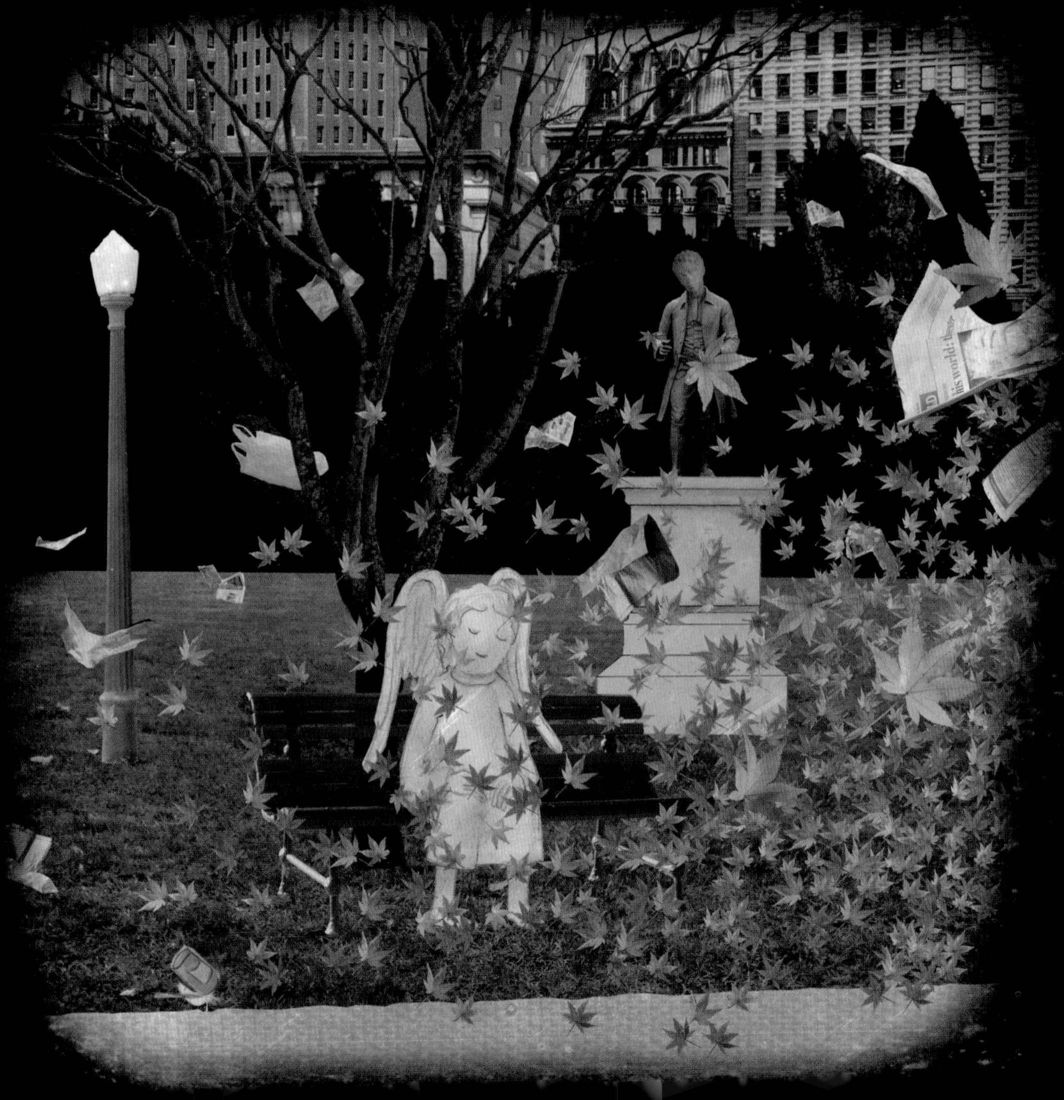

it appears, like a statue

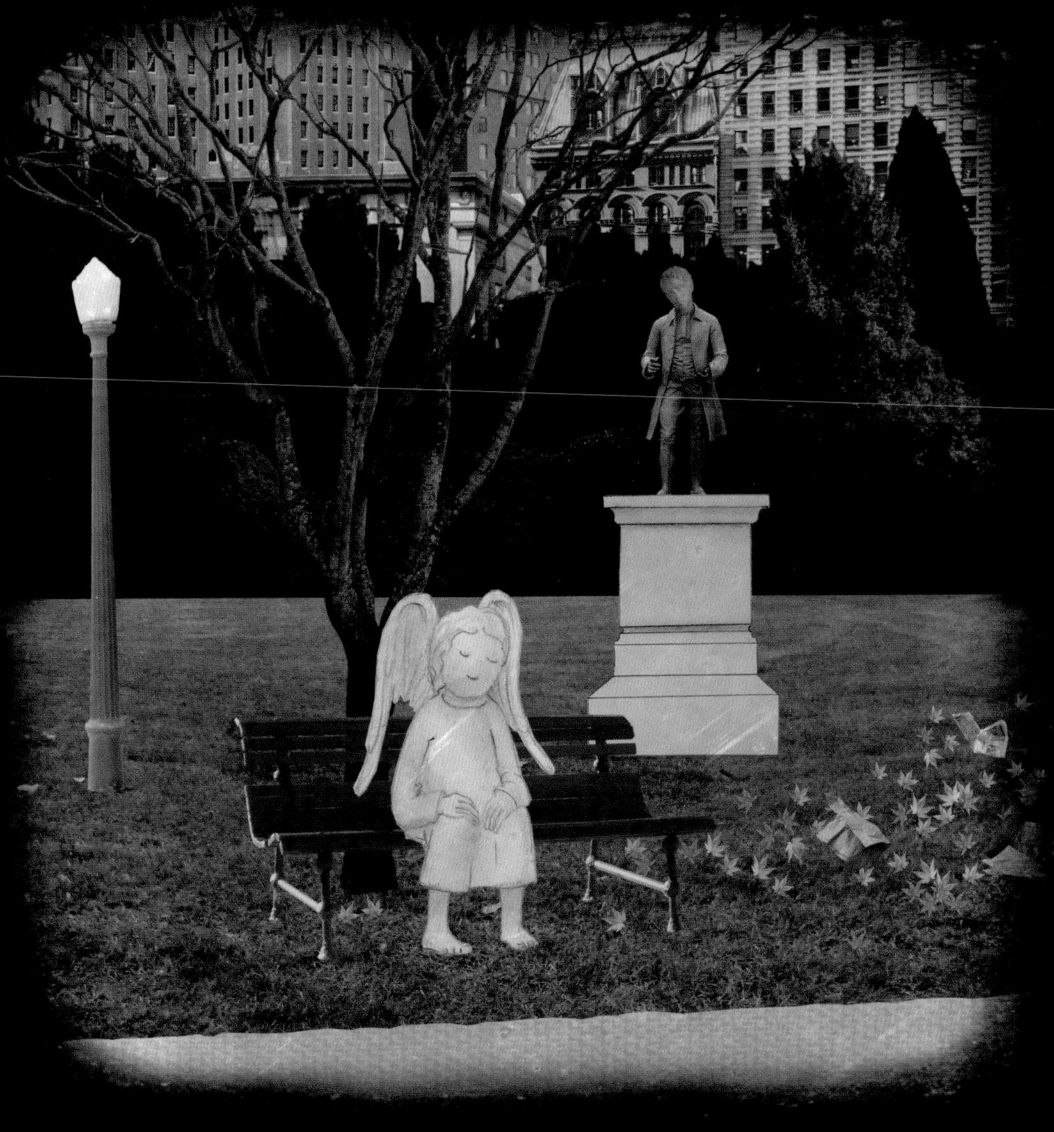

for all to see

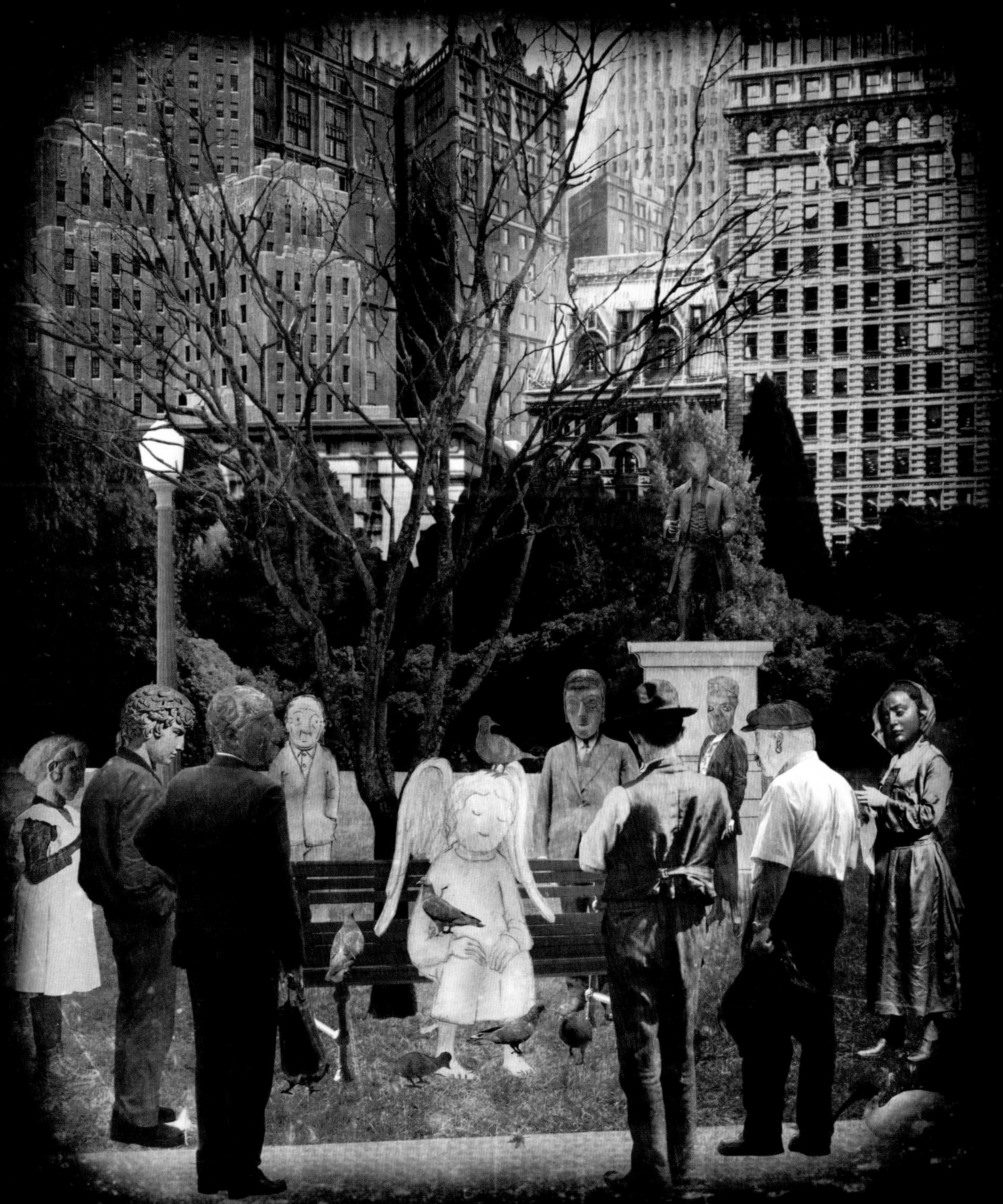

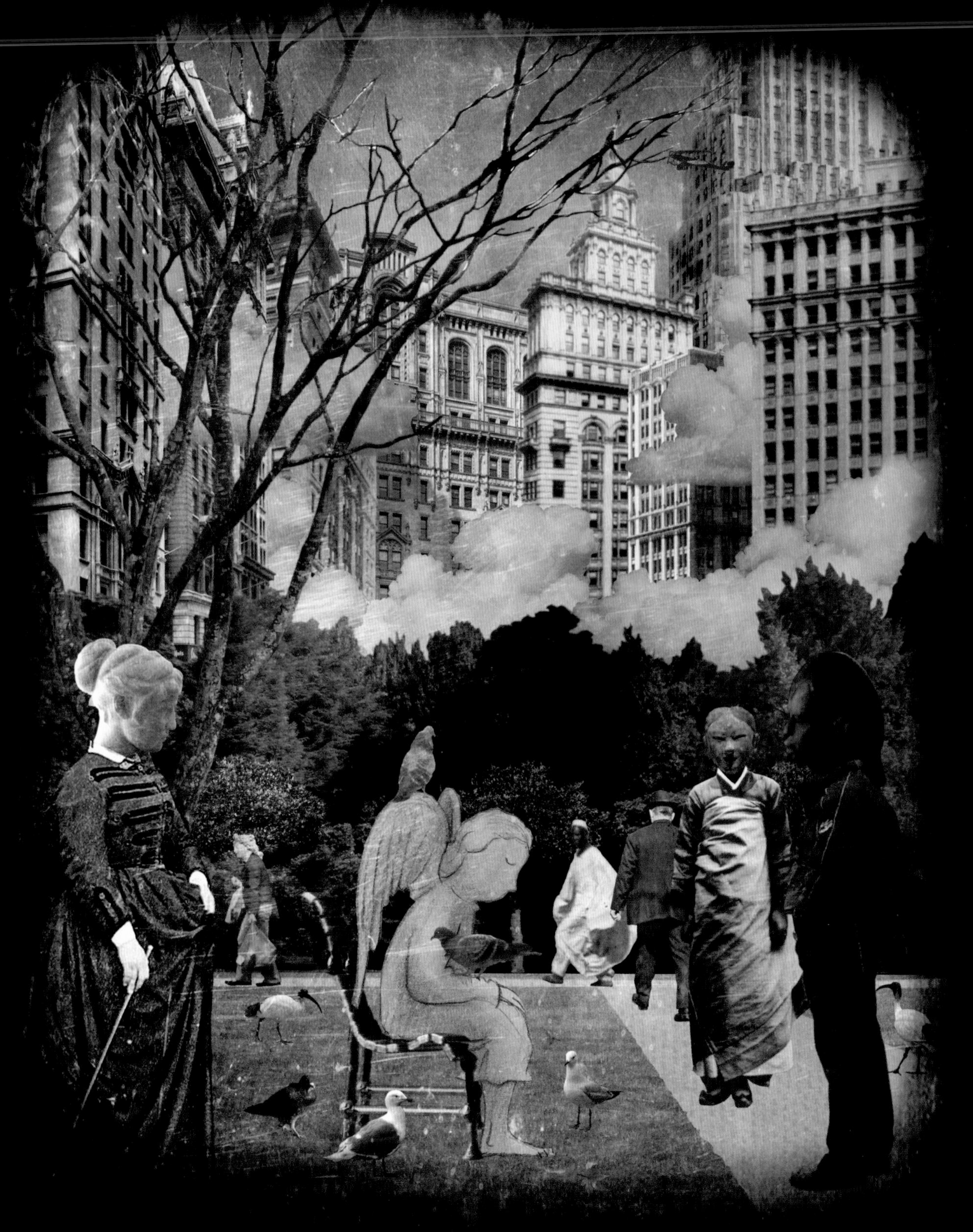

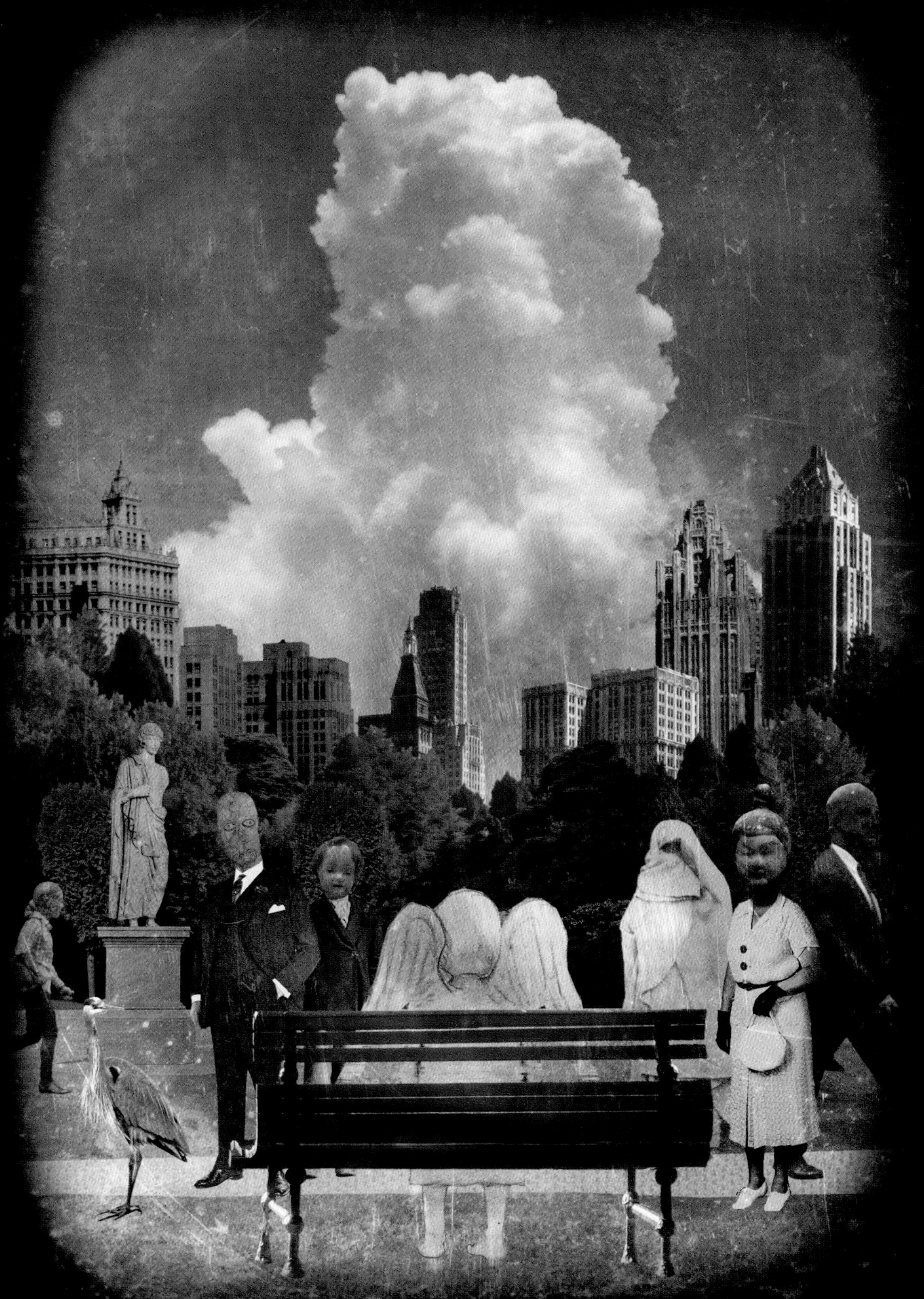

casting shadows in the light.

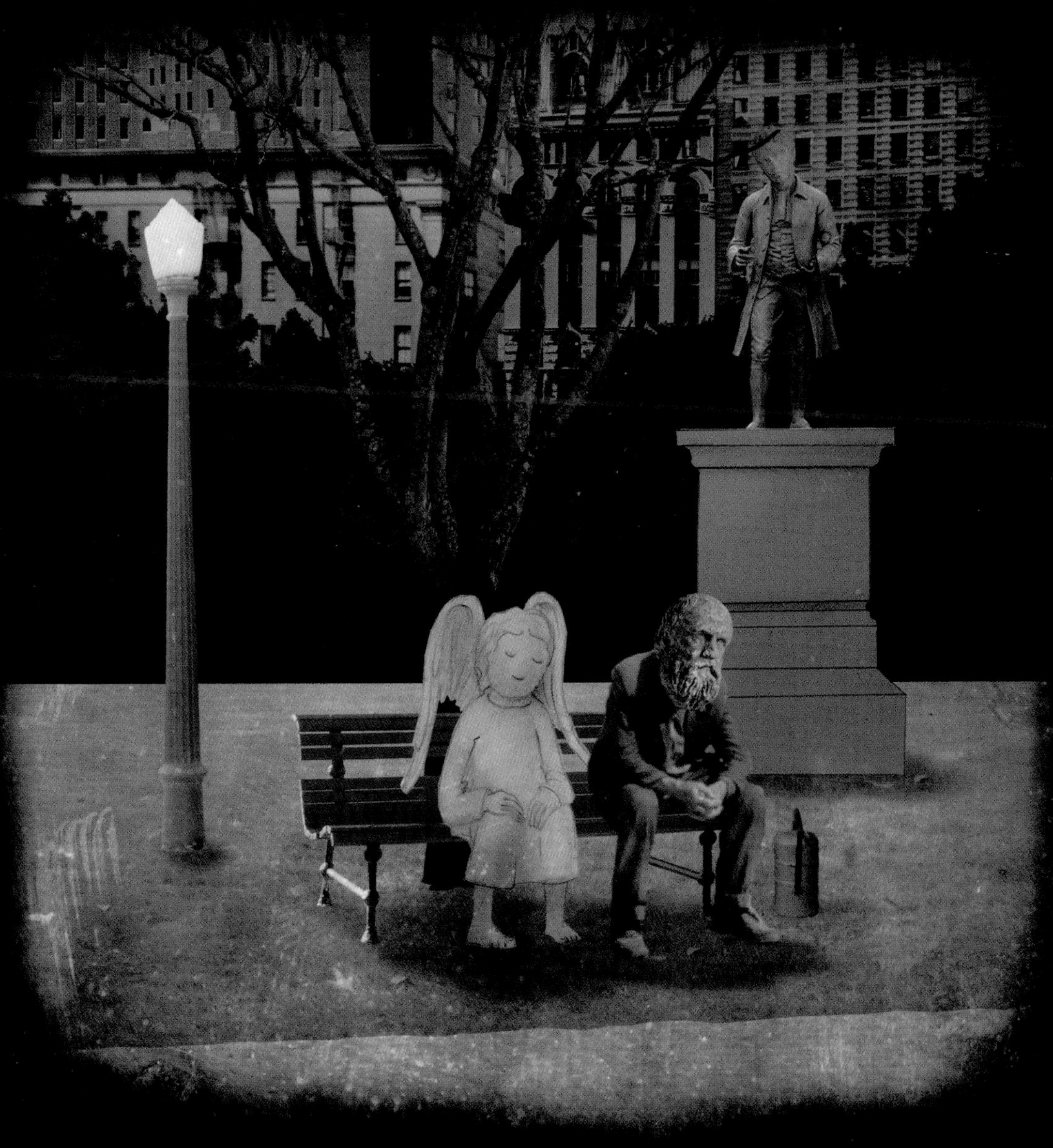

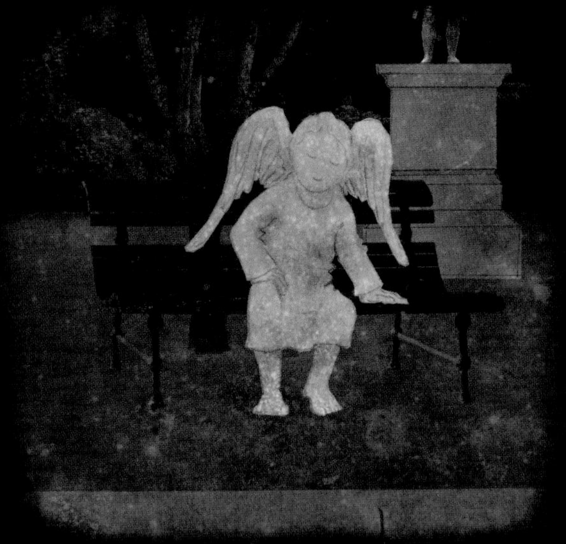
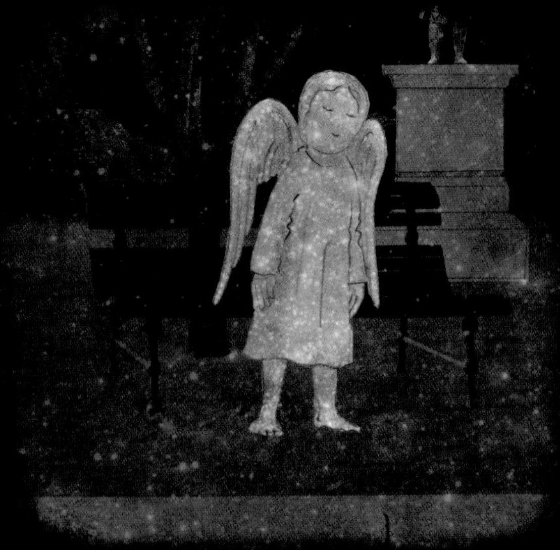
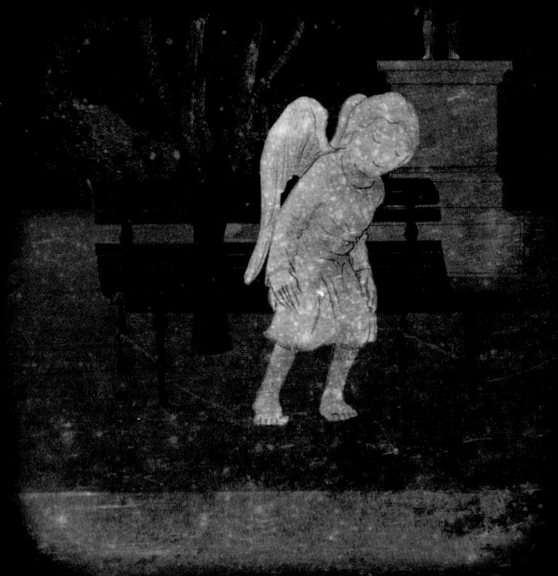
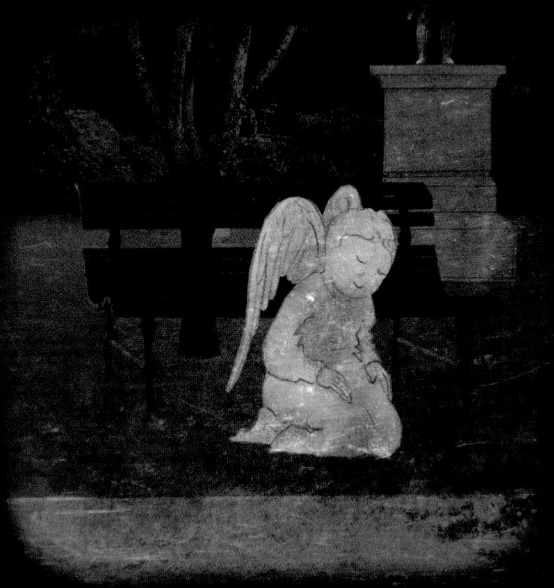

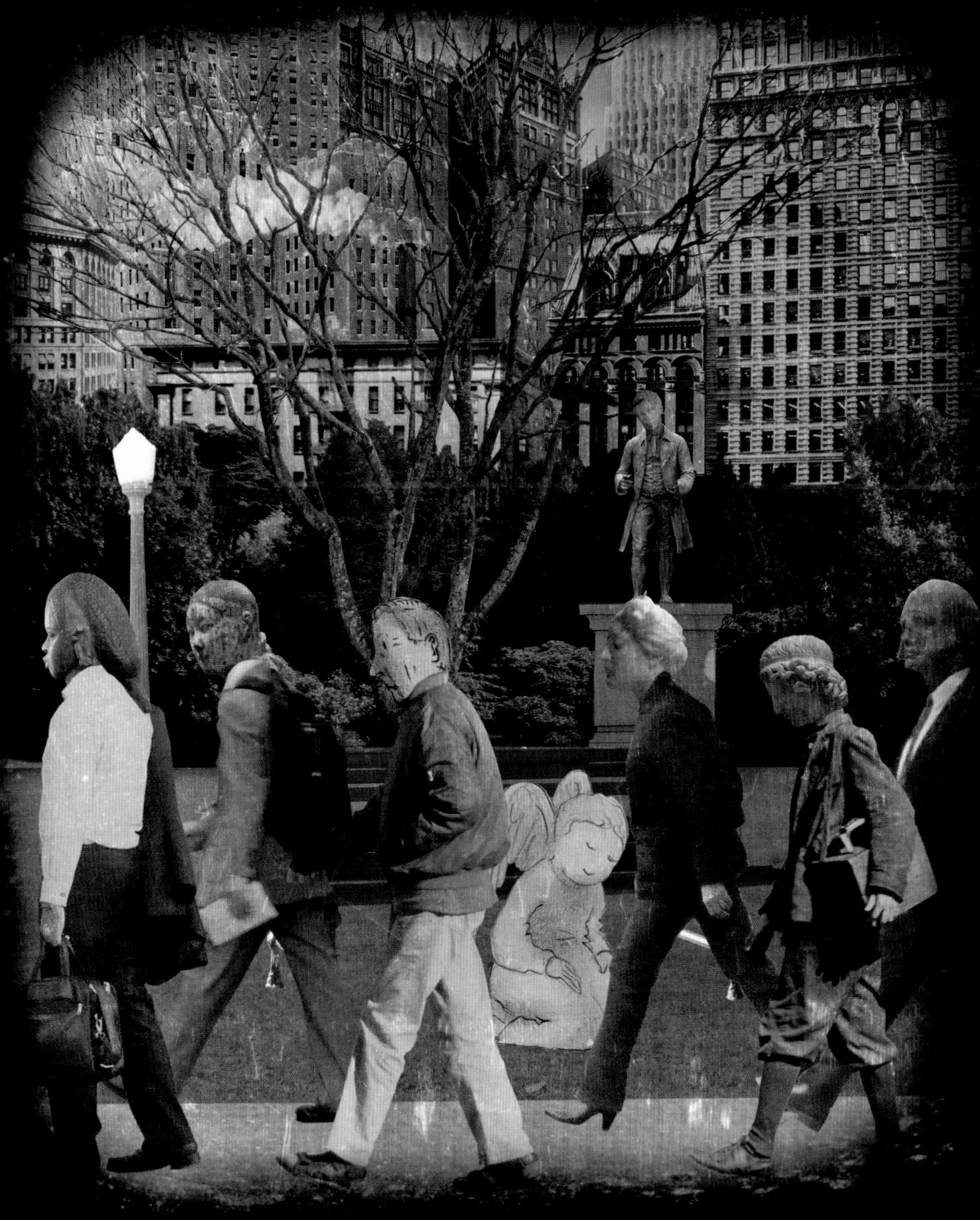

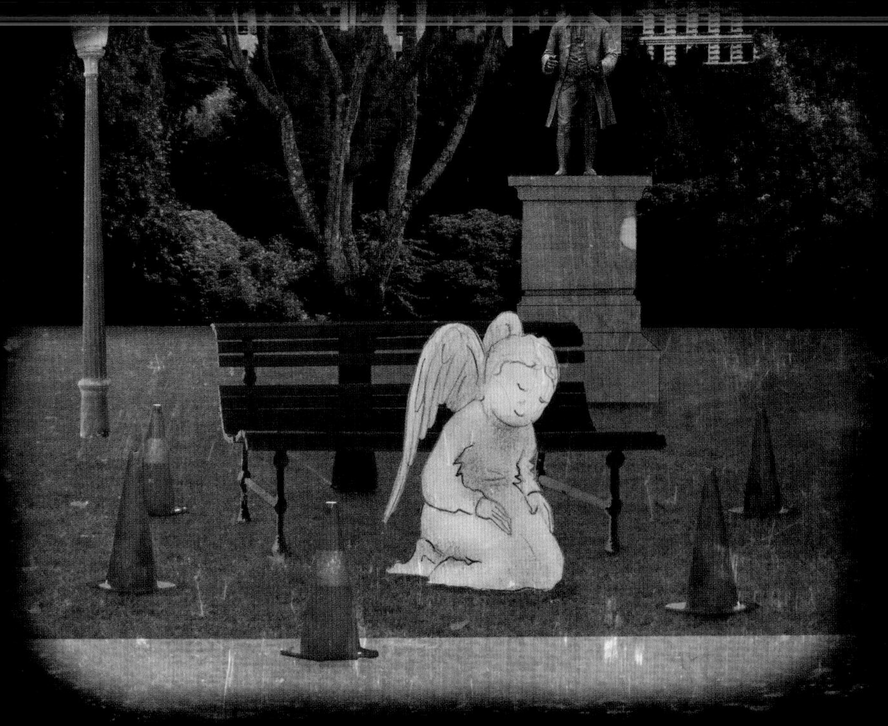

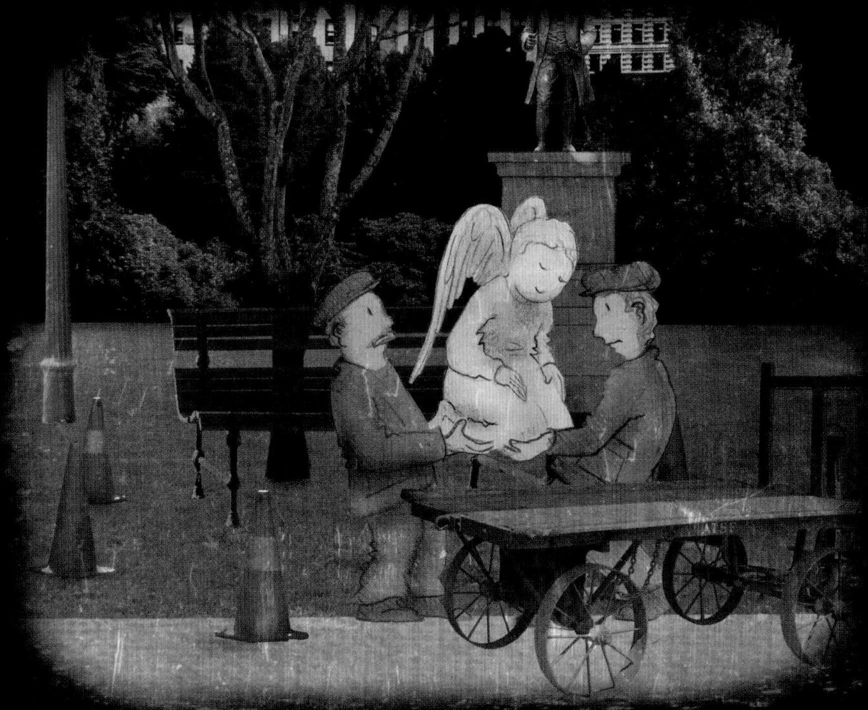

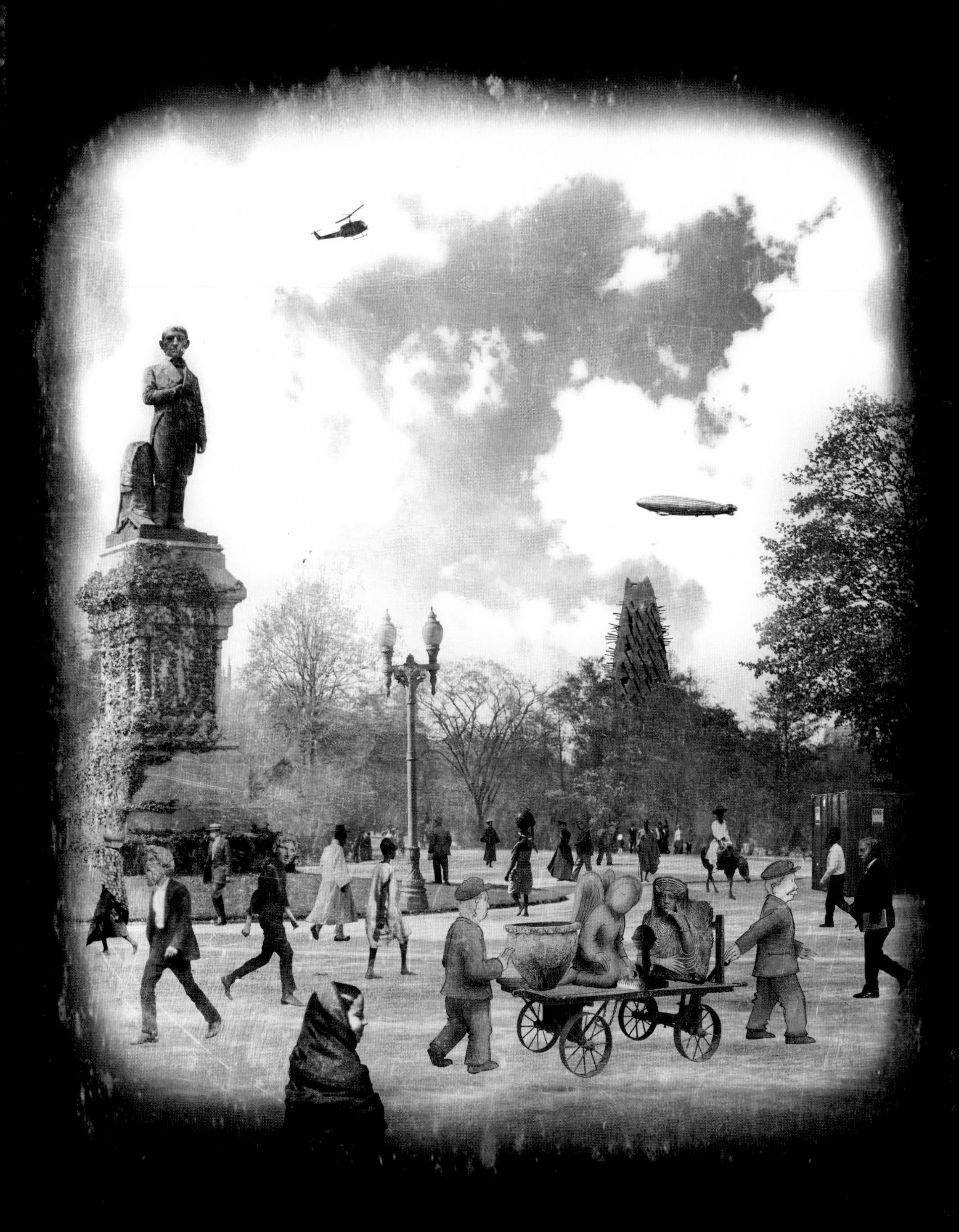

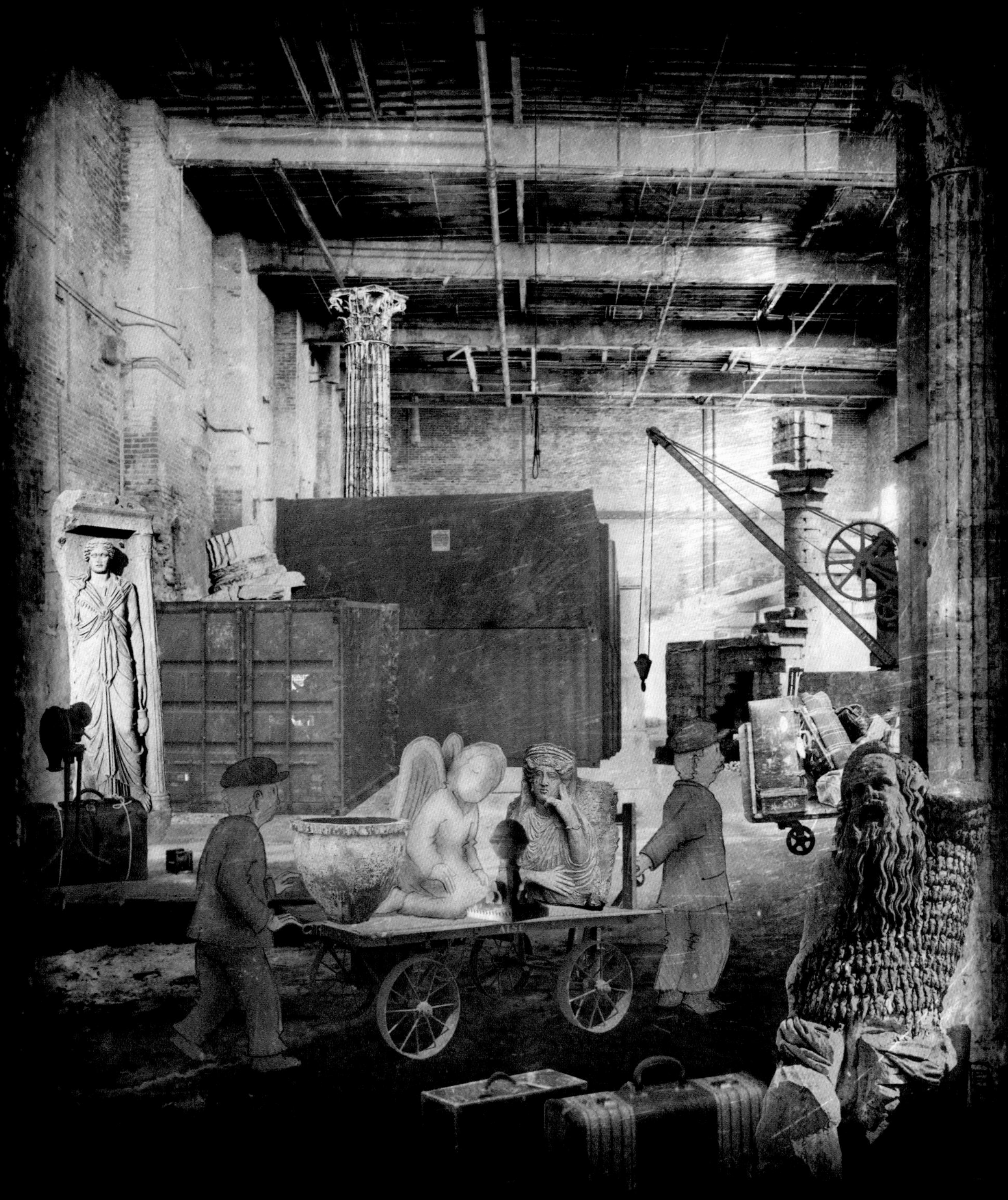

Finally, it is given a resting place.

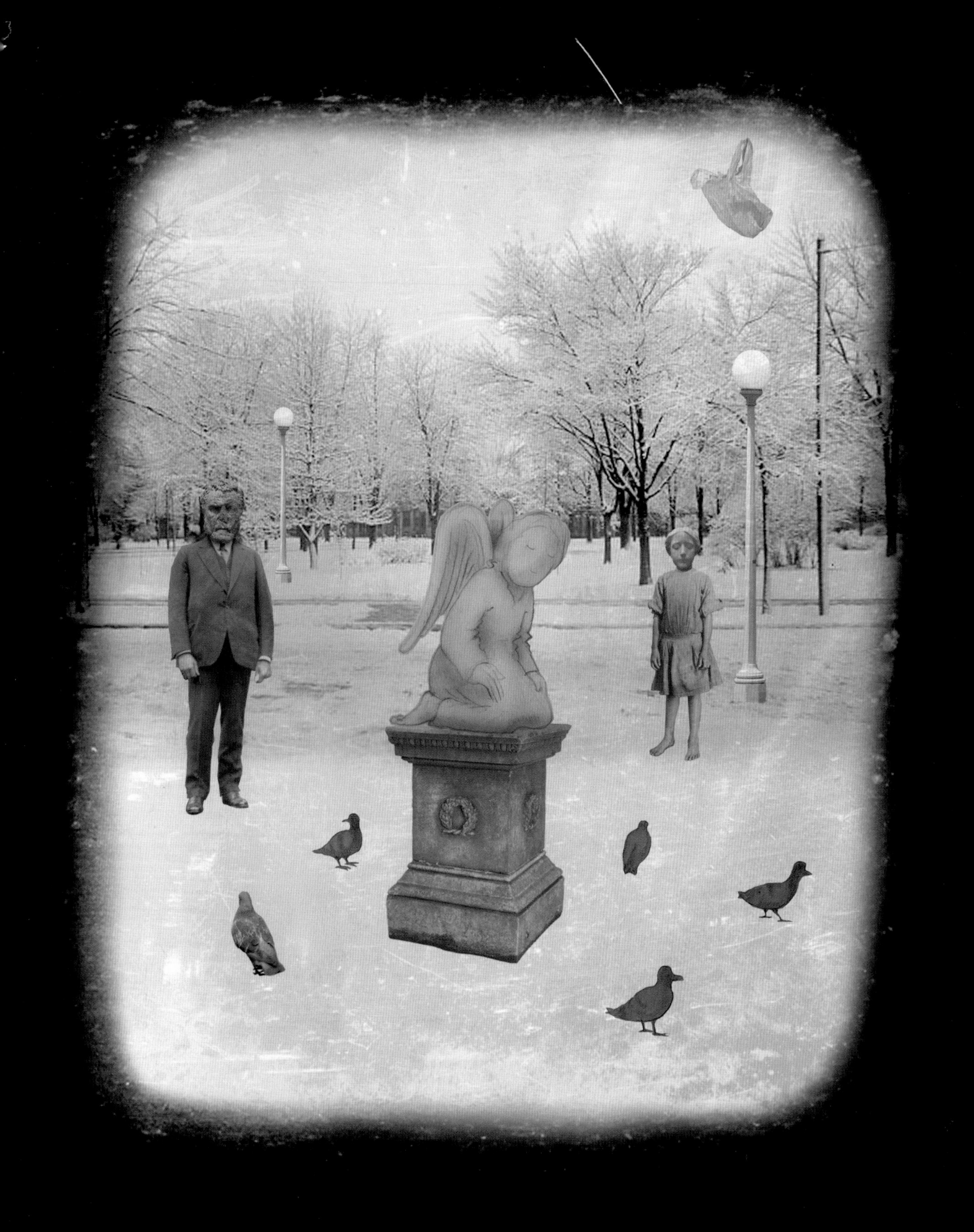

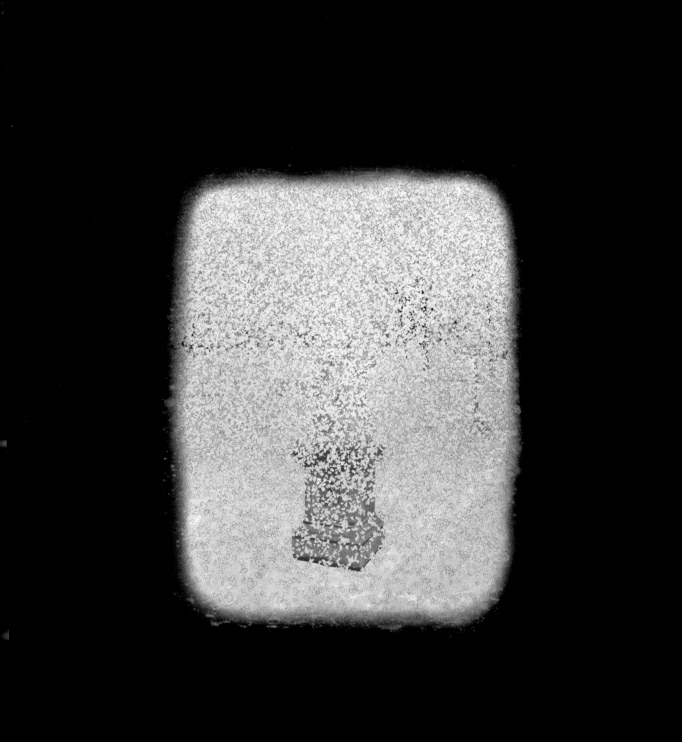

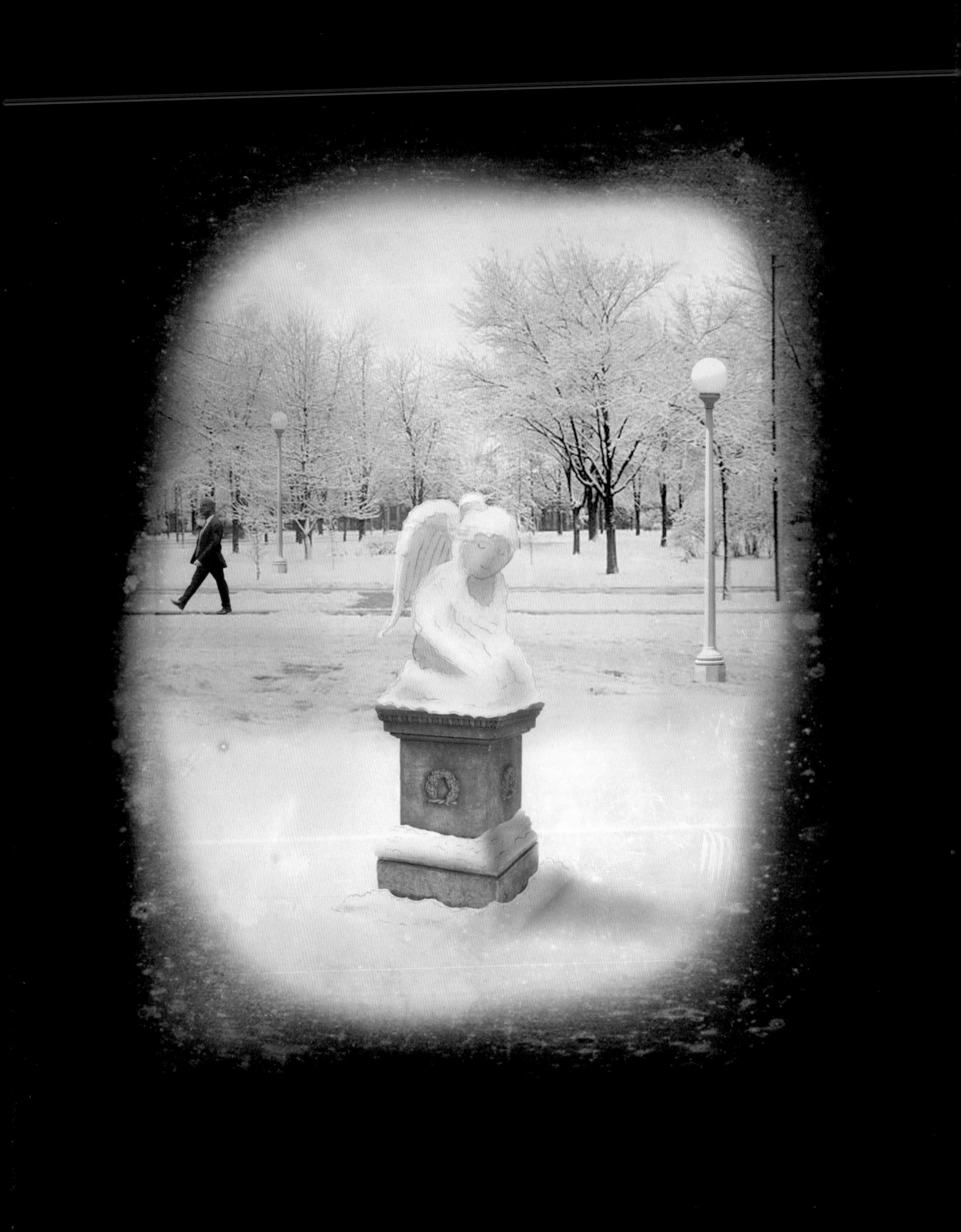

III

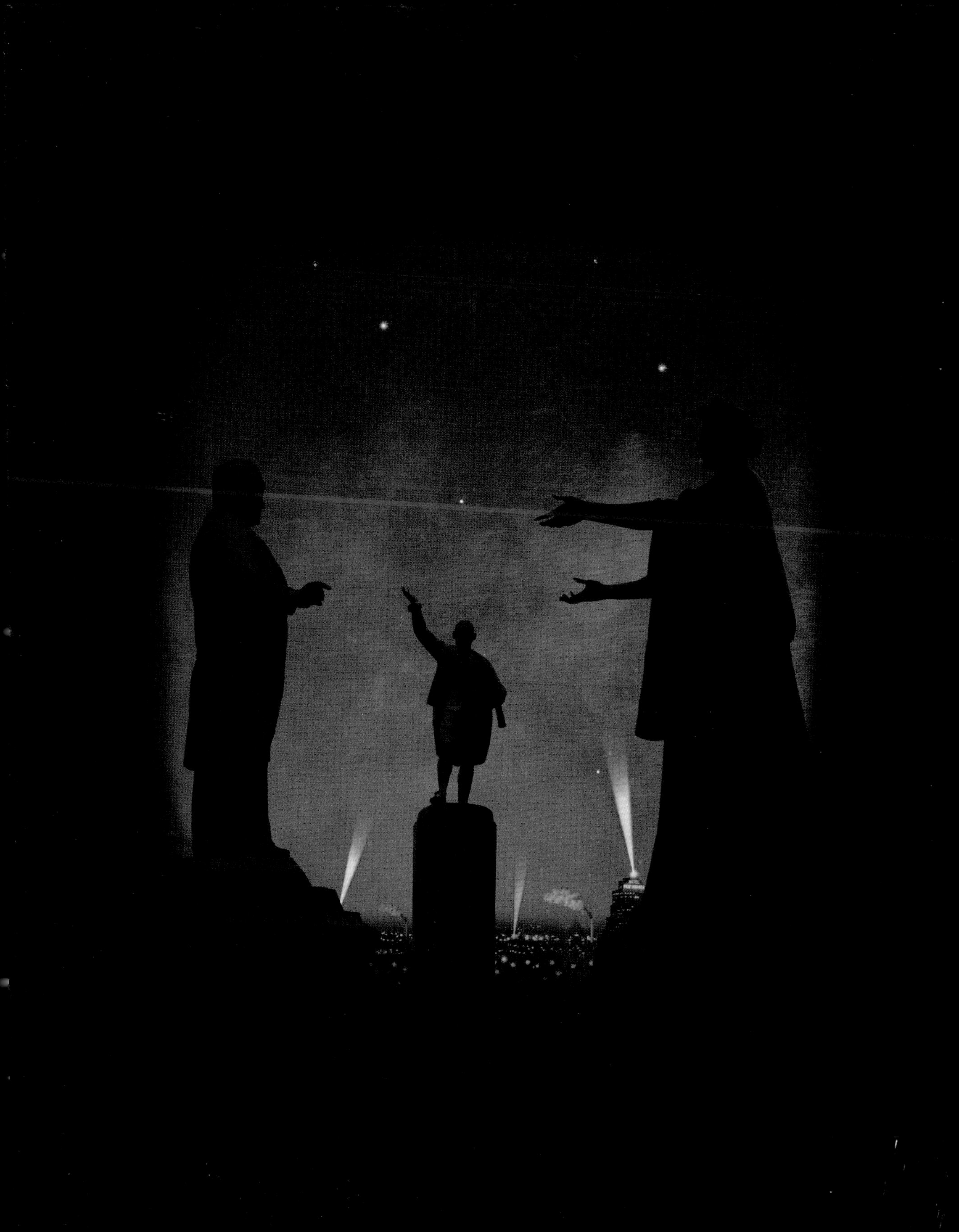

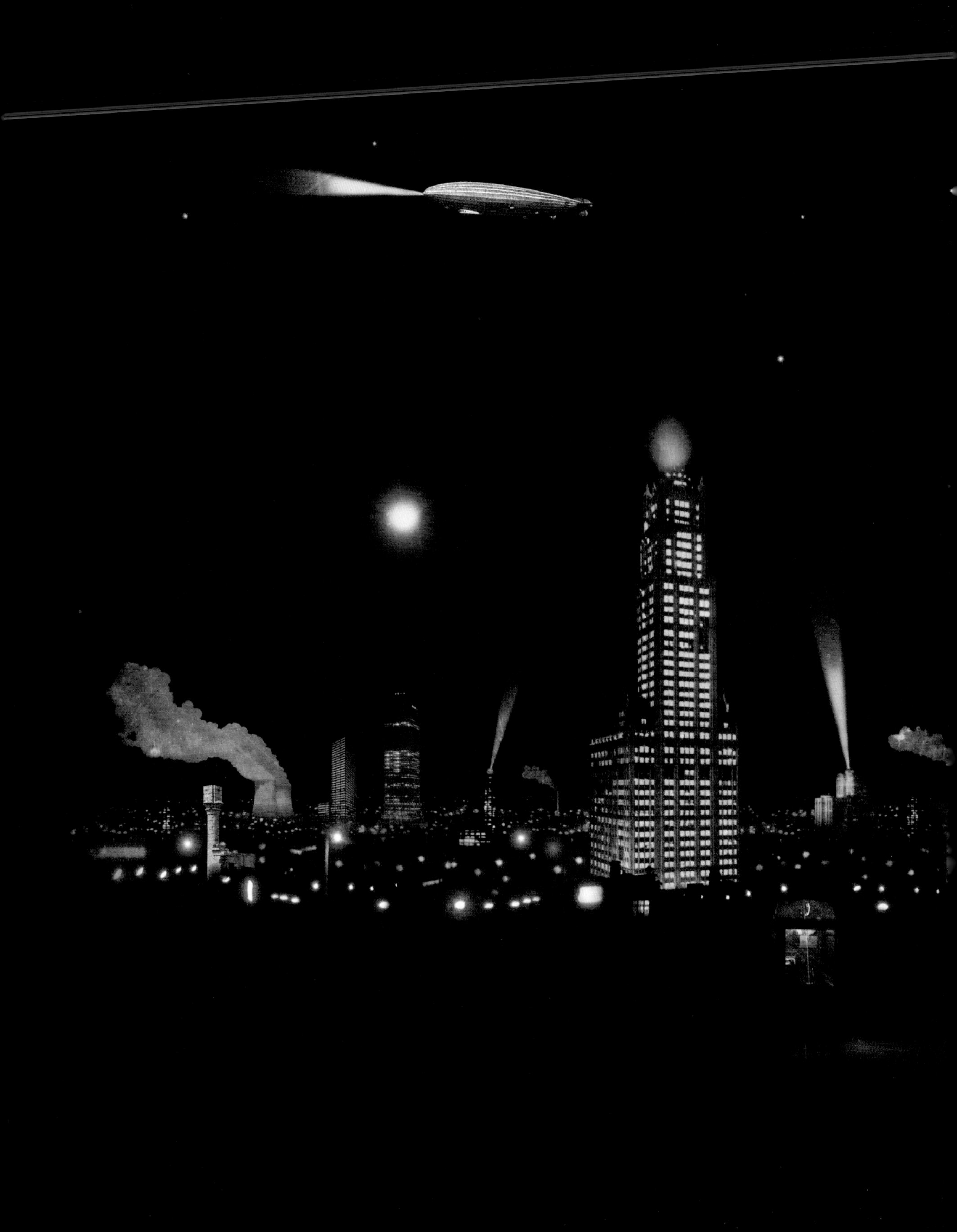

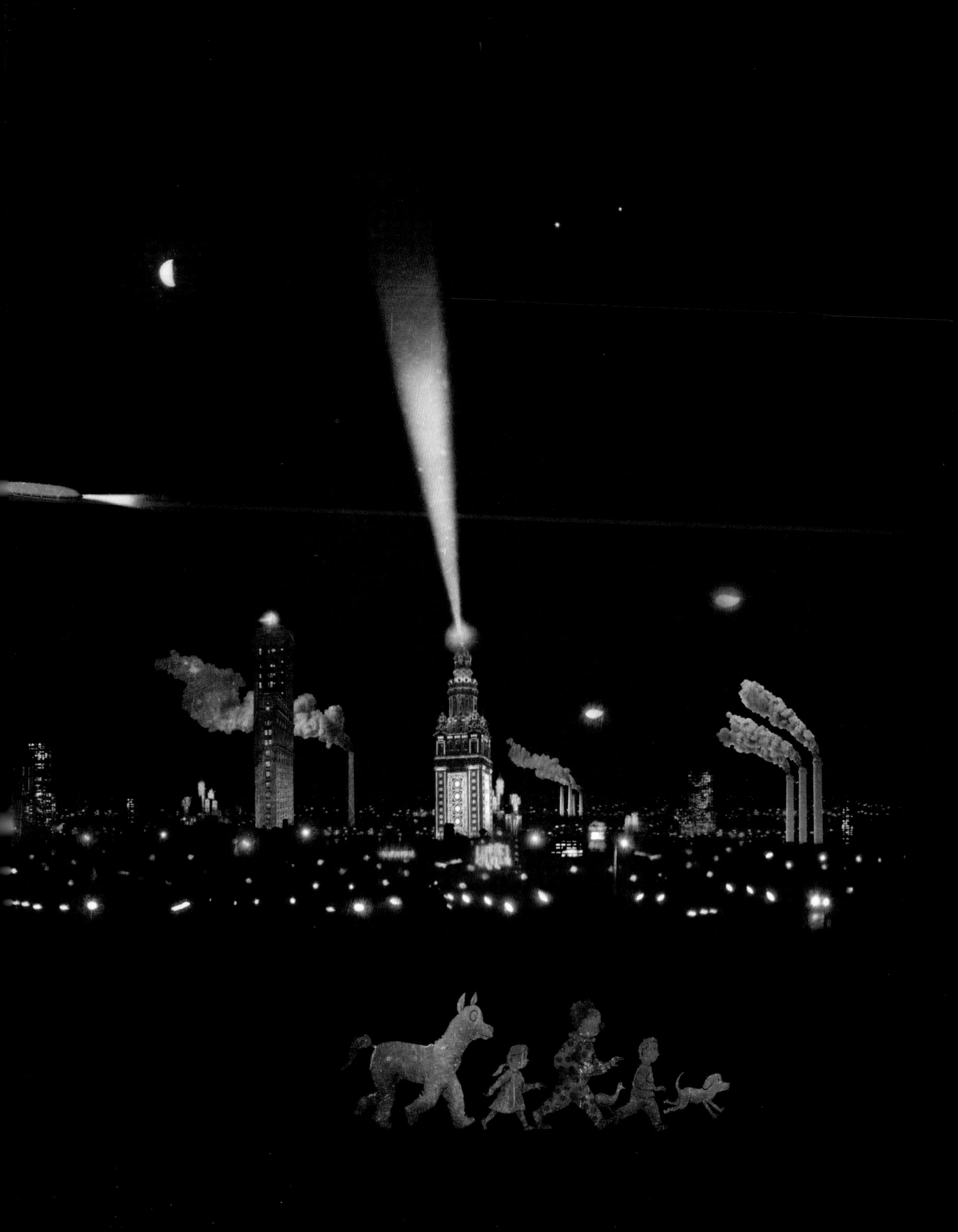

But before it can move no more

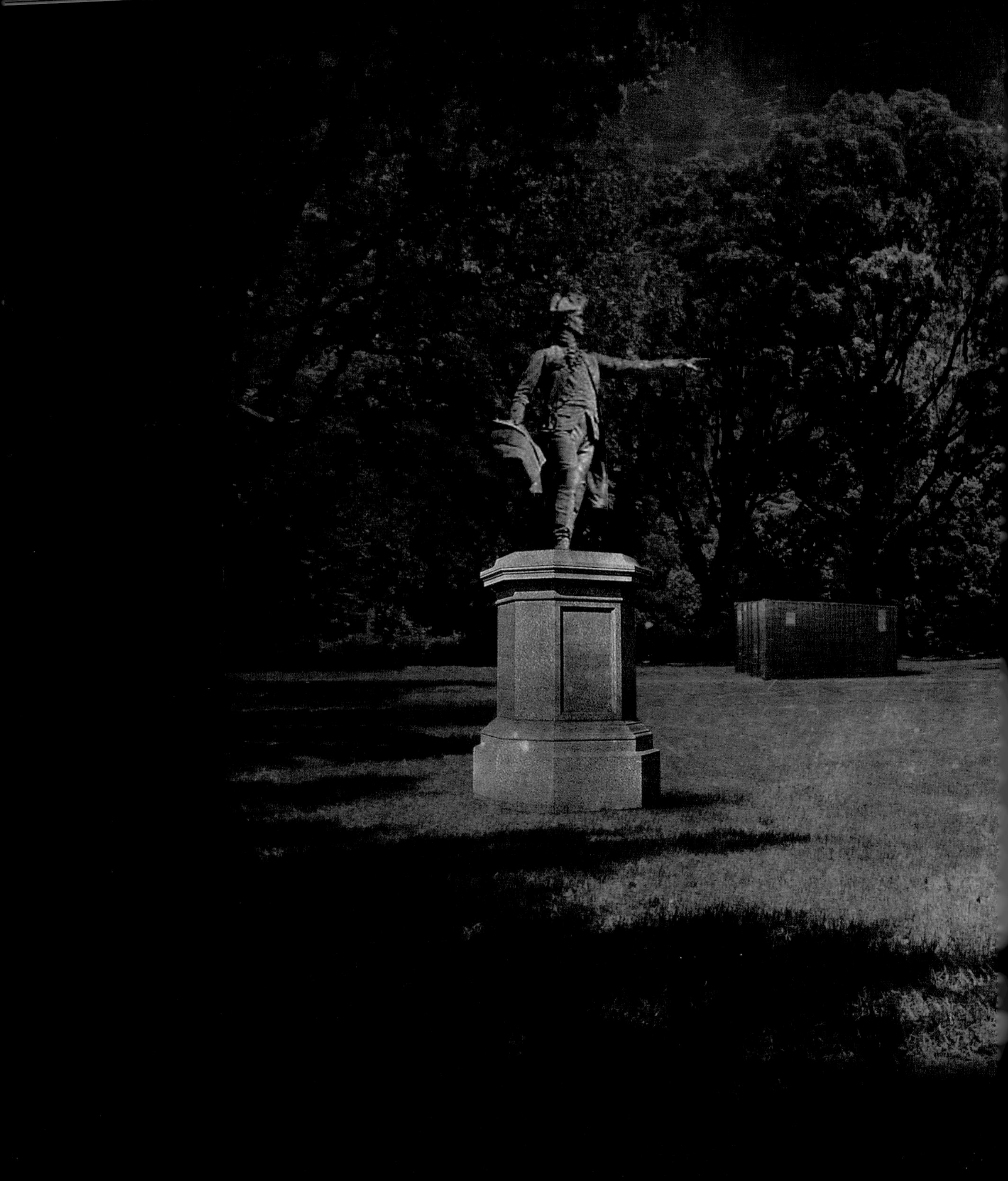

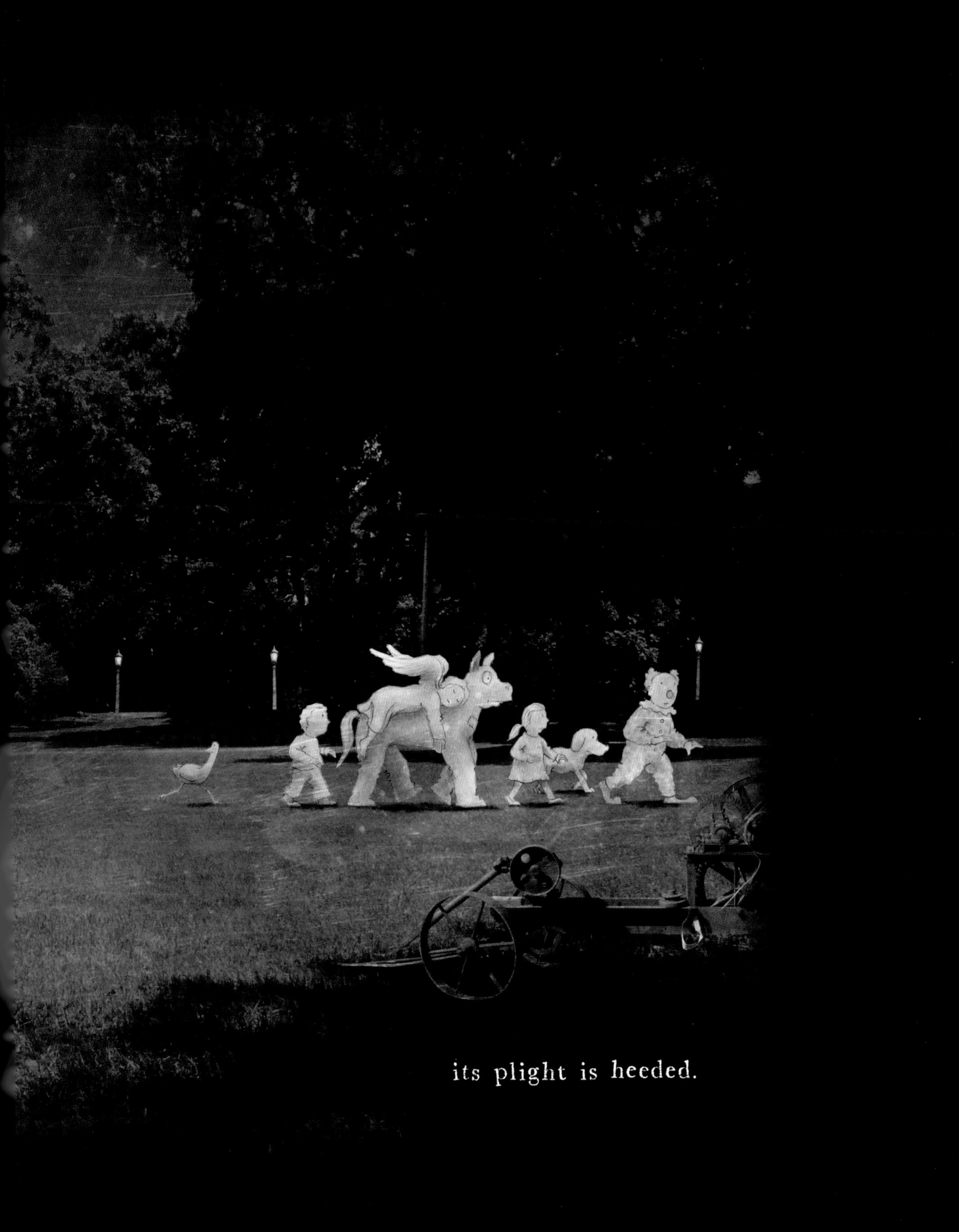

its plight is heeded.

GARAGE

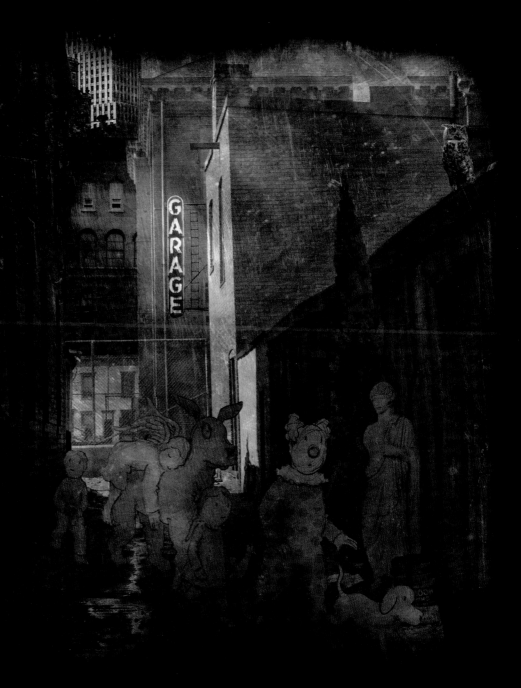

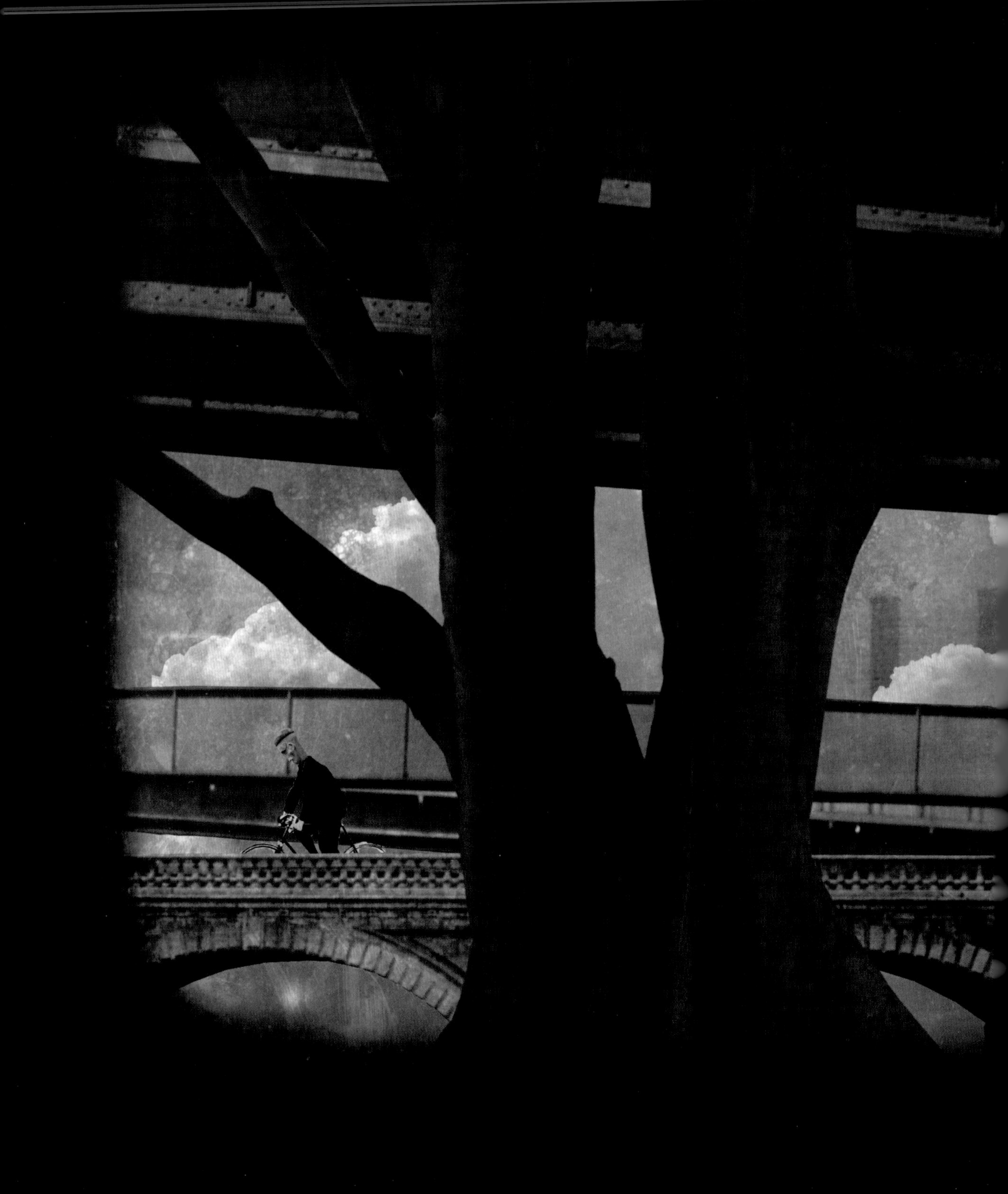

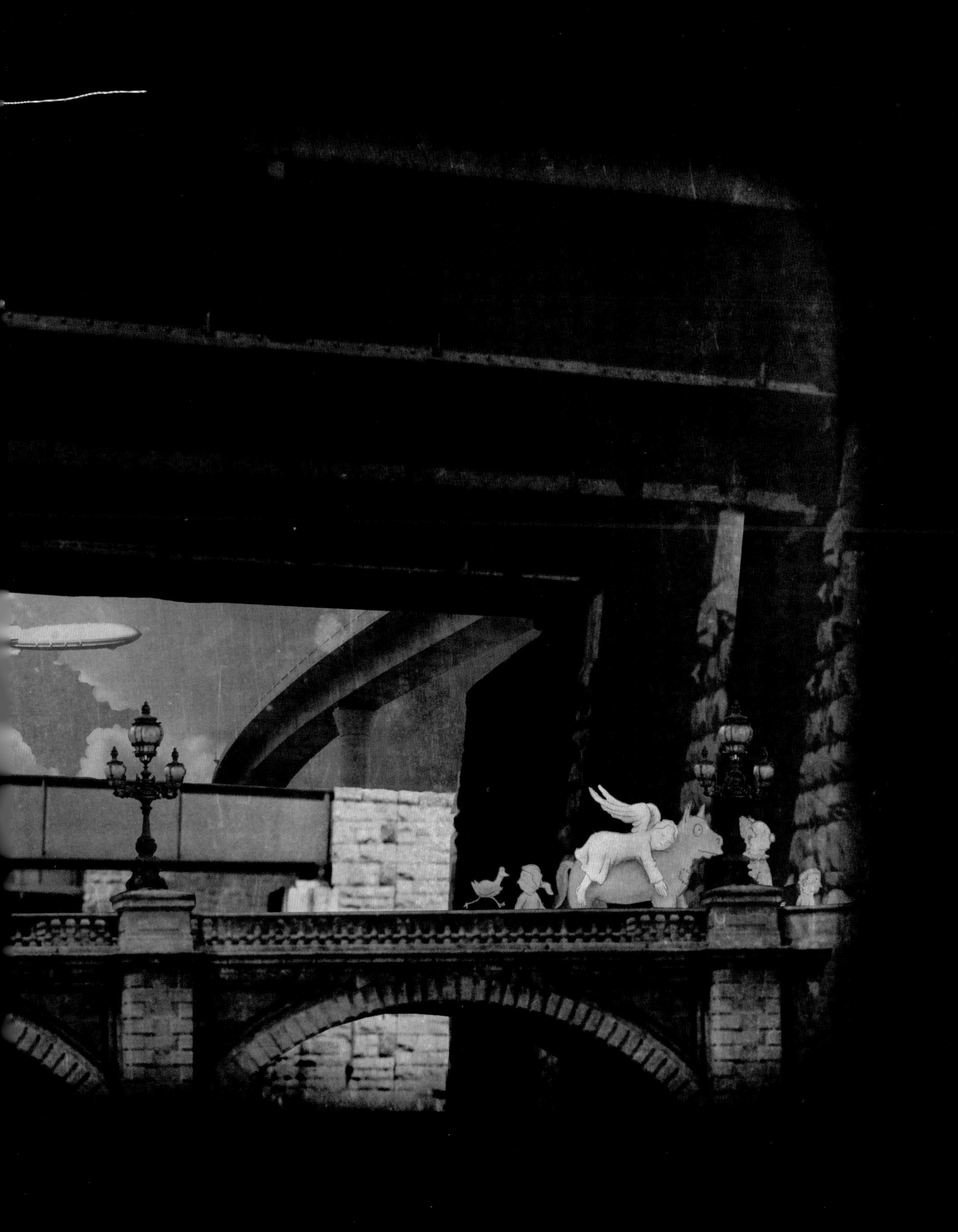

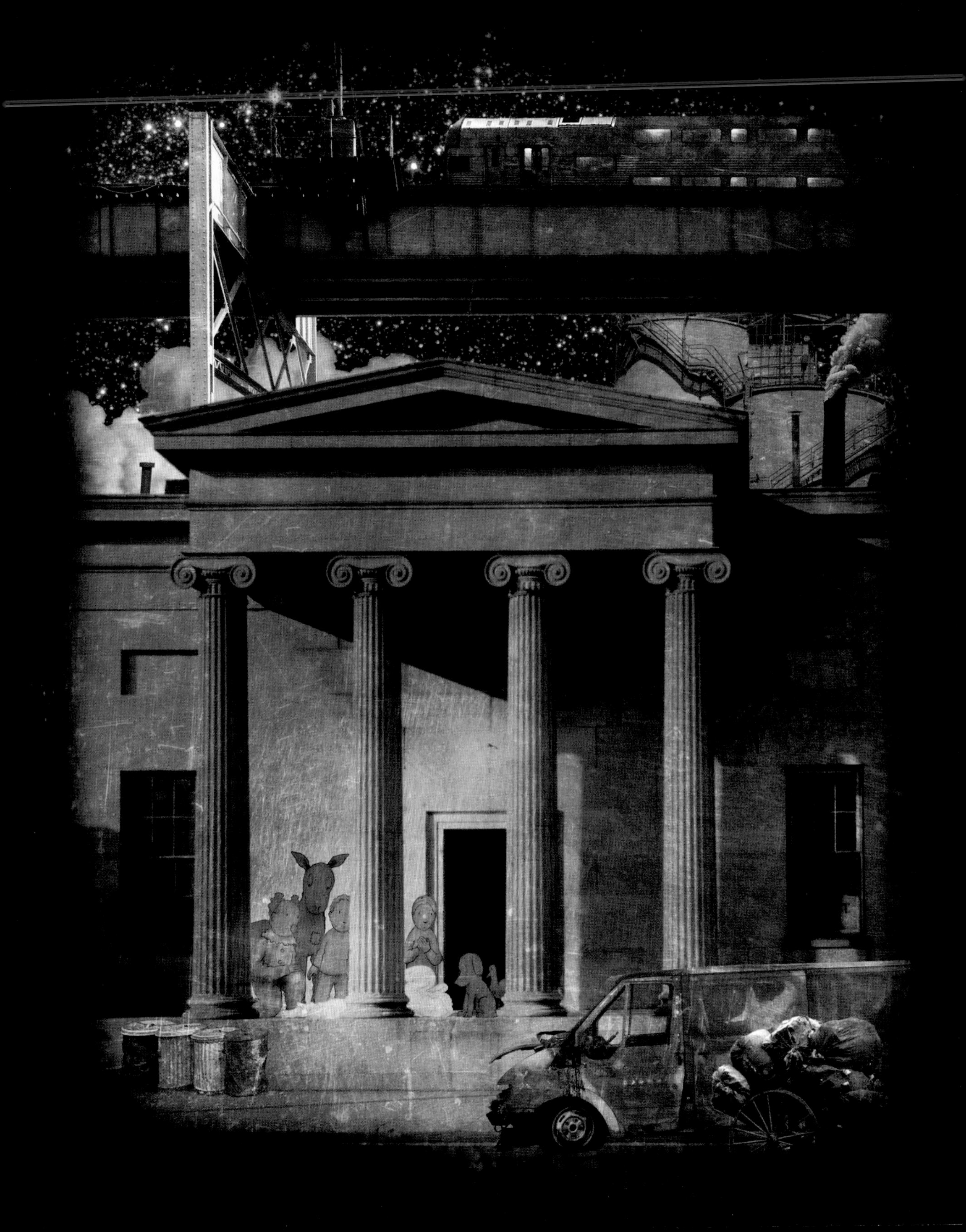

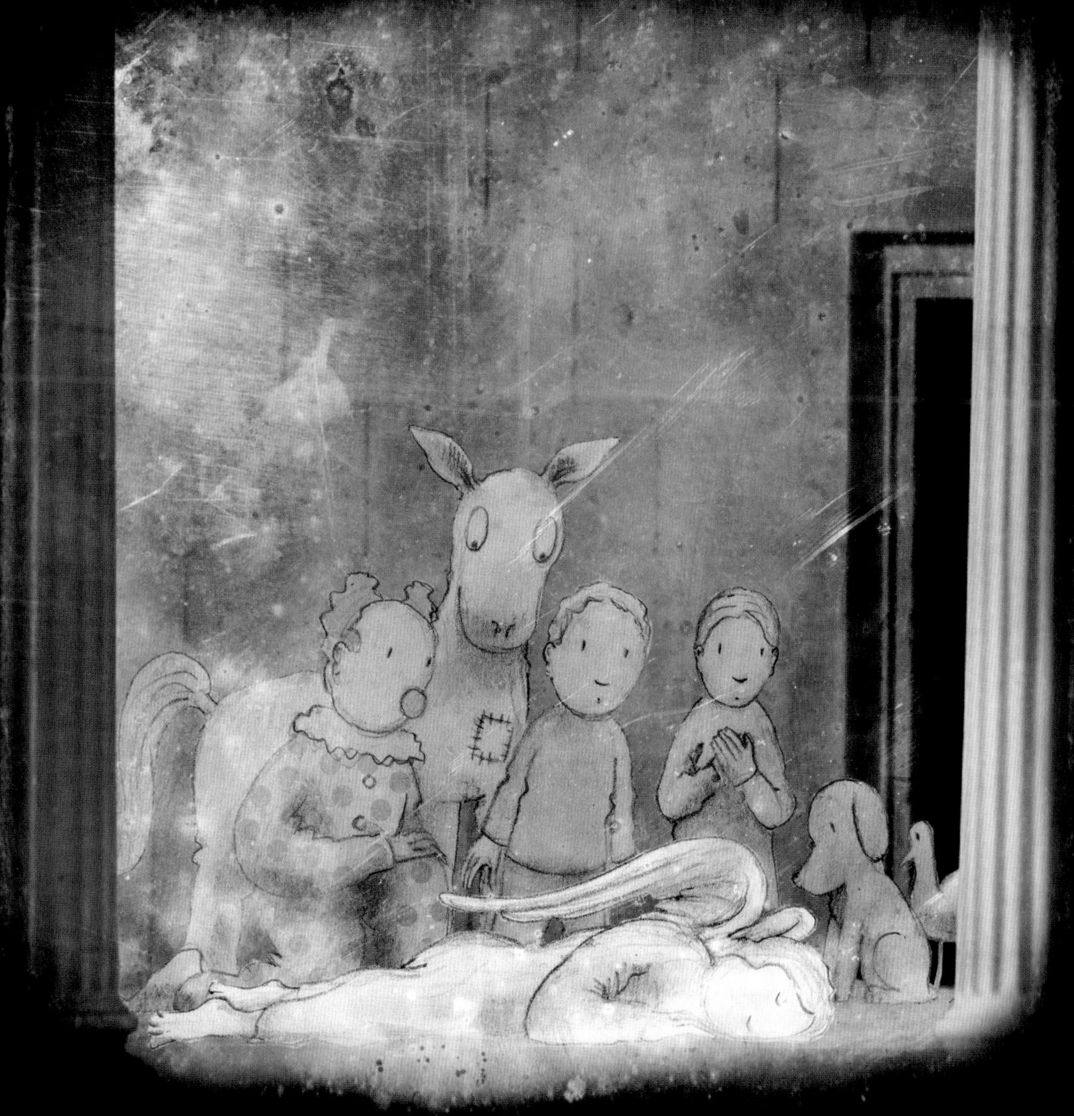

And it is watched over

and warmed

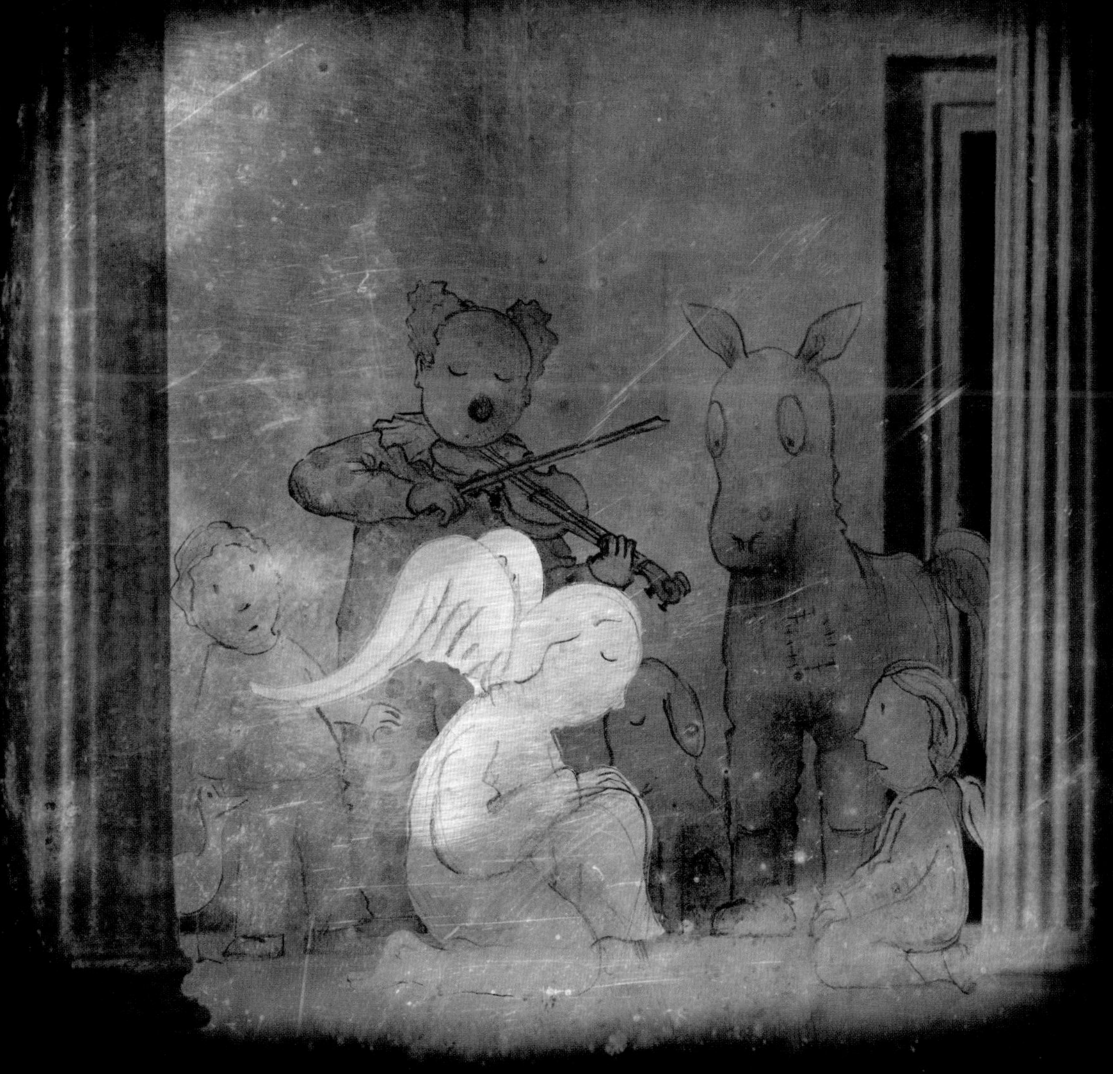

and mended.

And where it goes

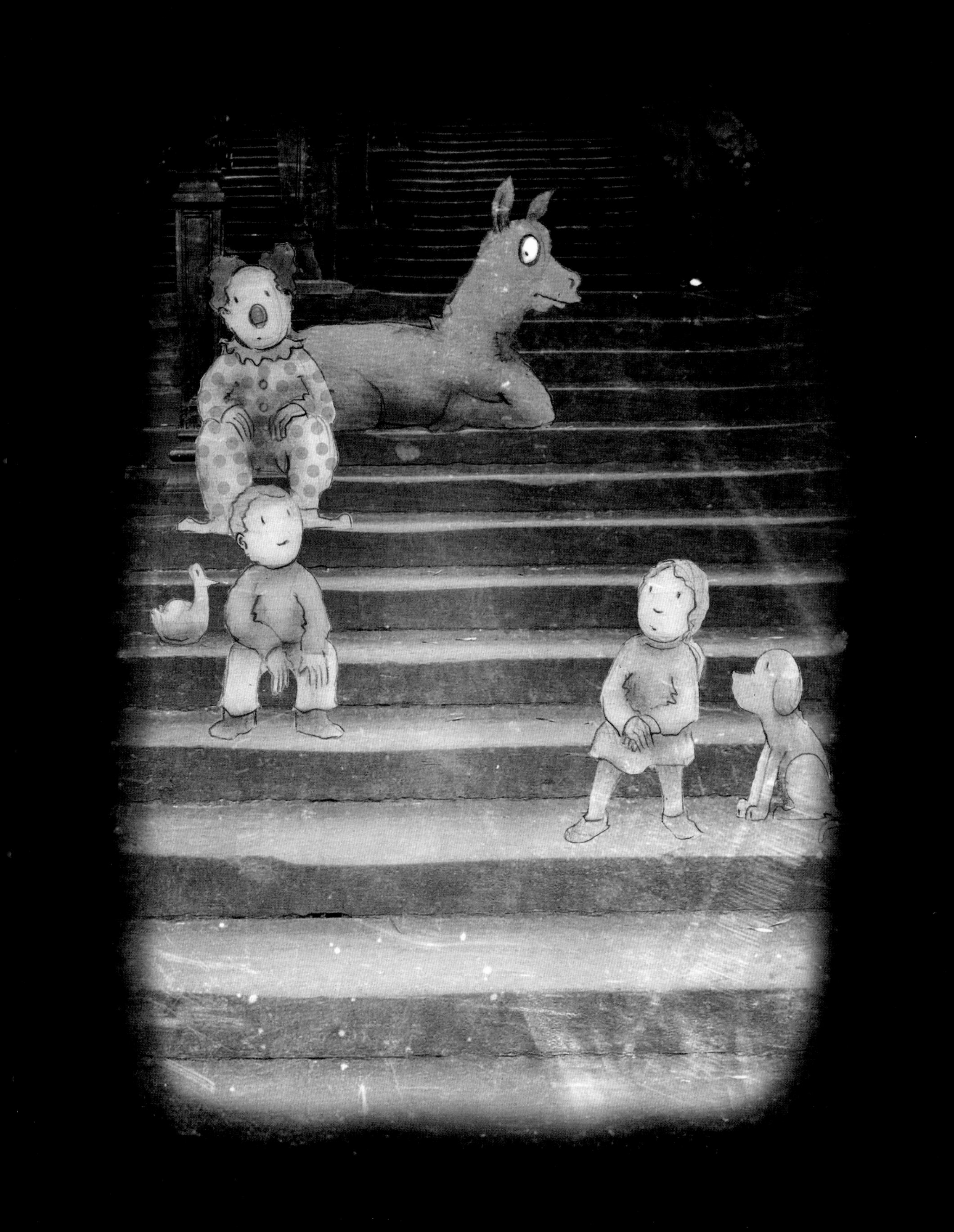

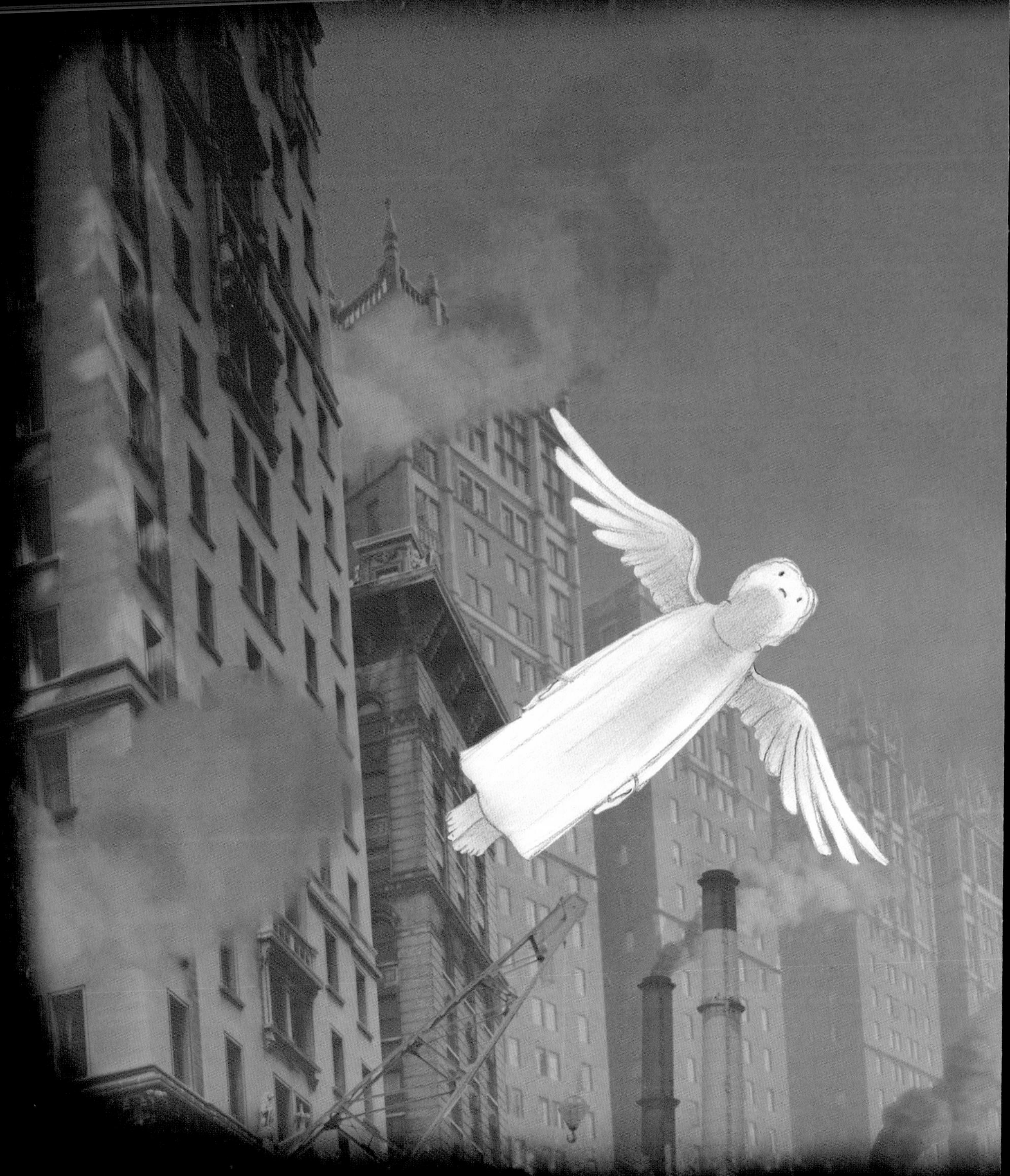

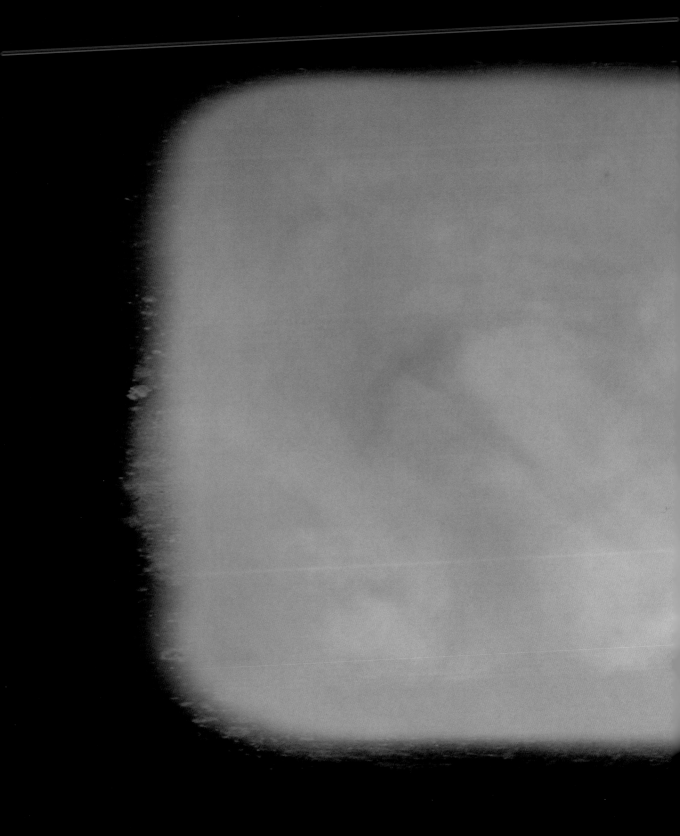

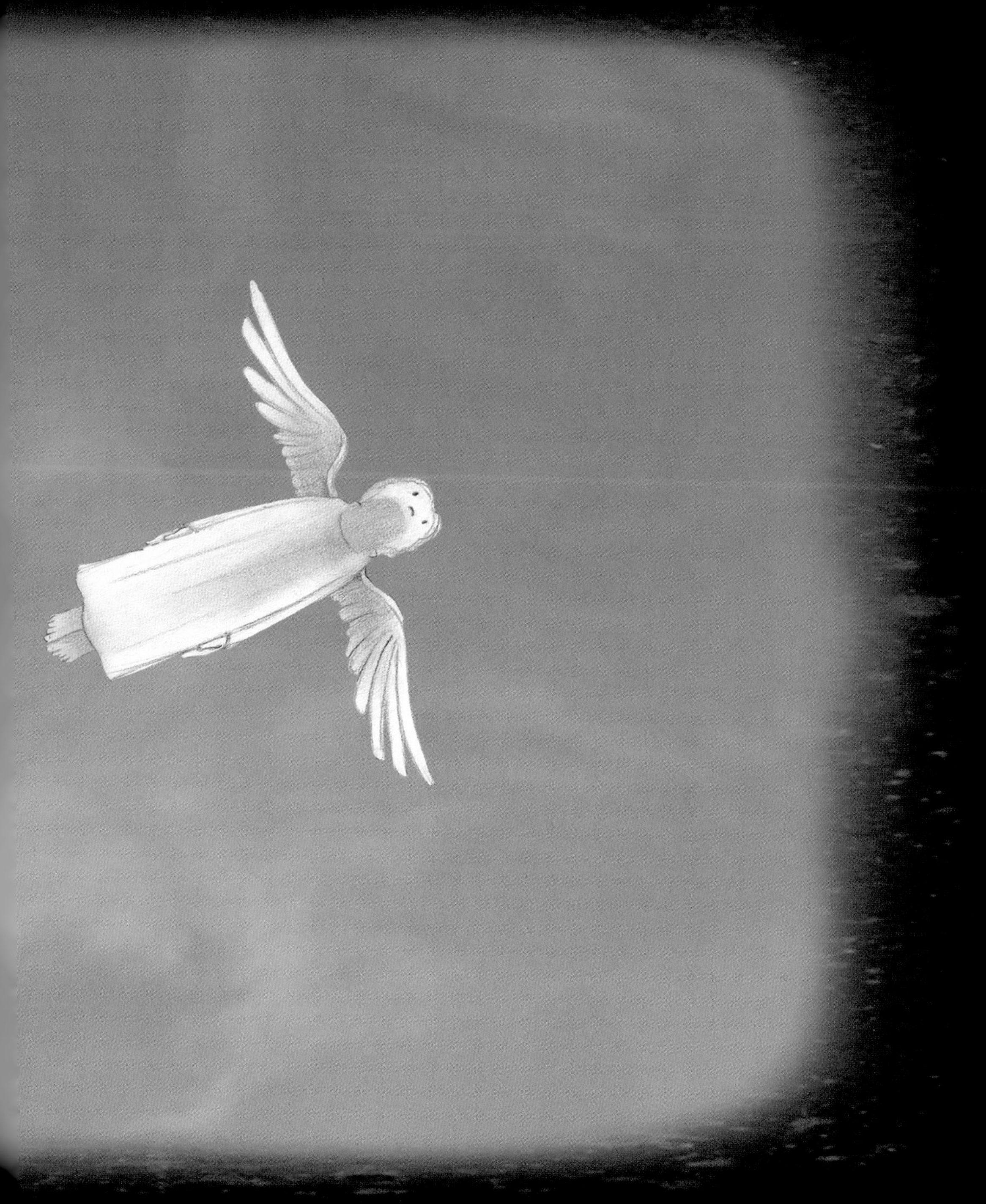

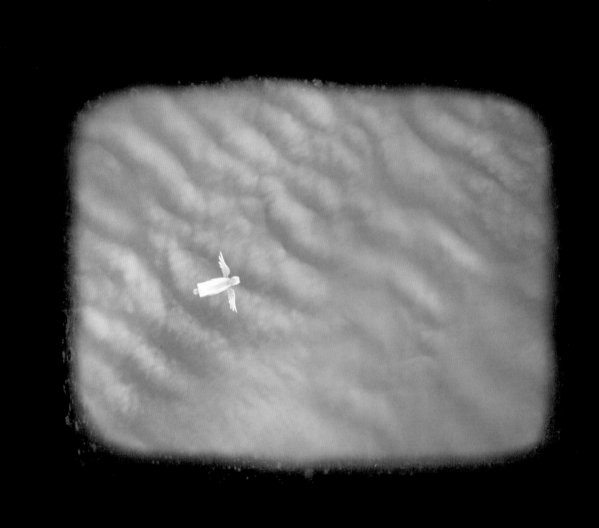

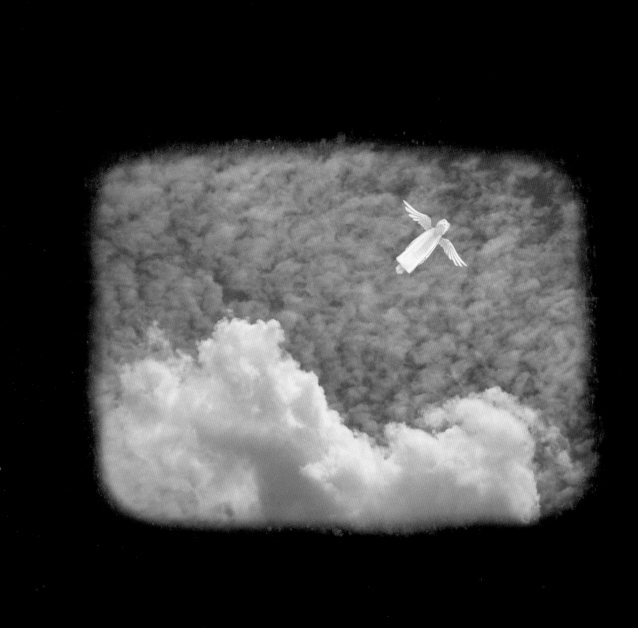

nobody knows.

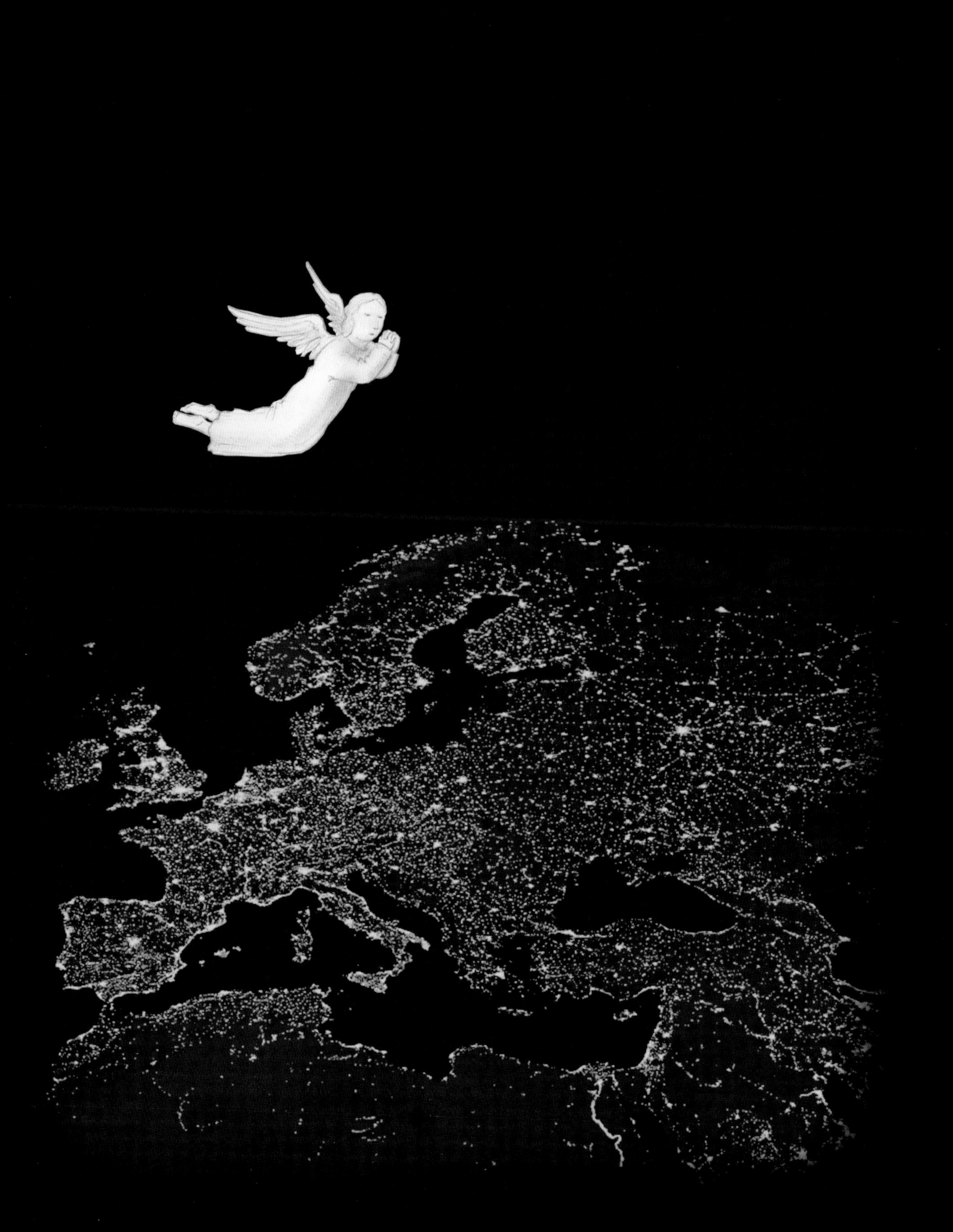

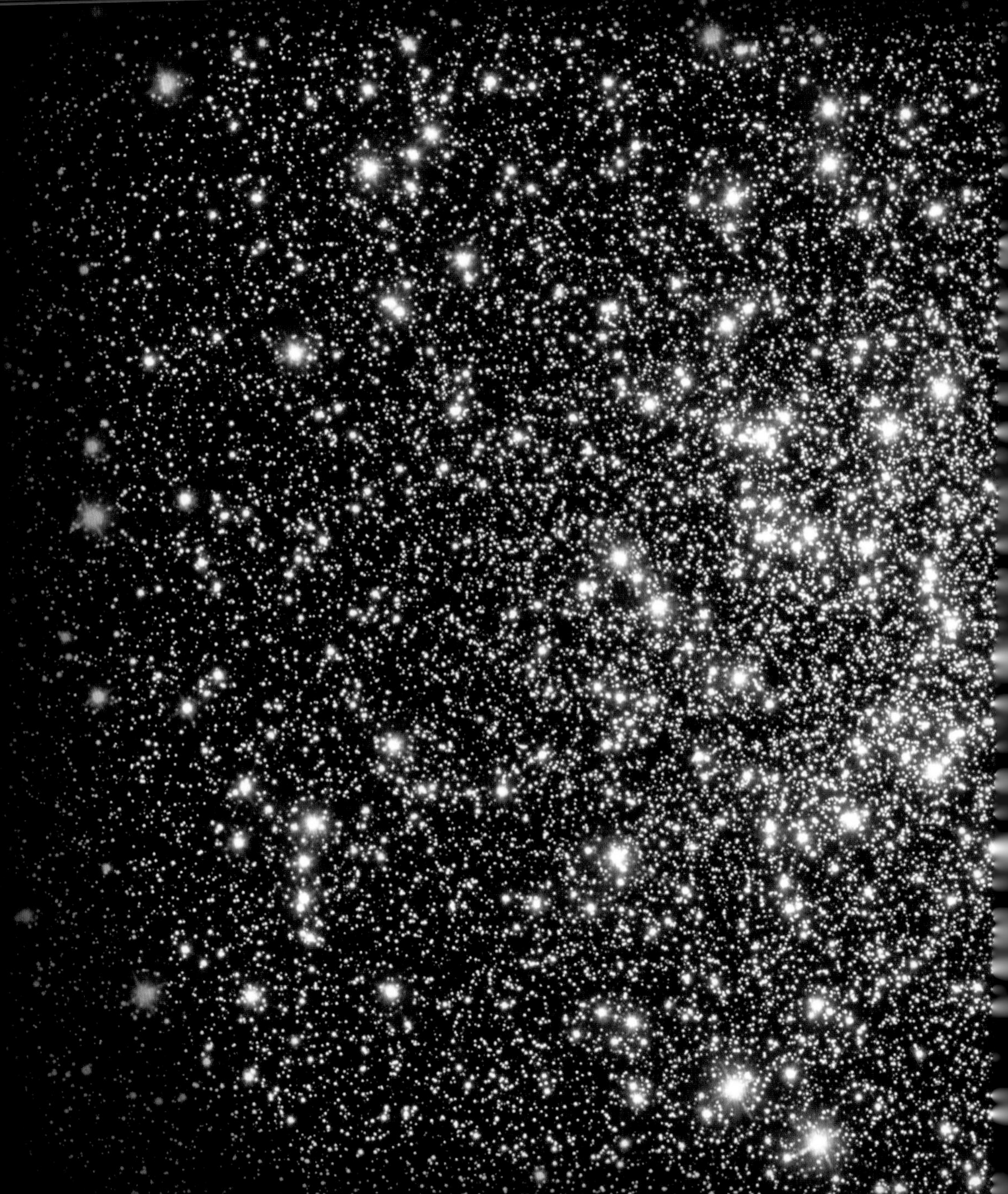

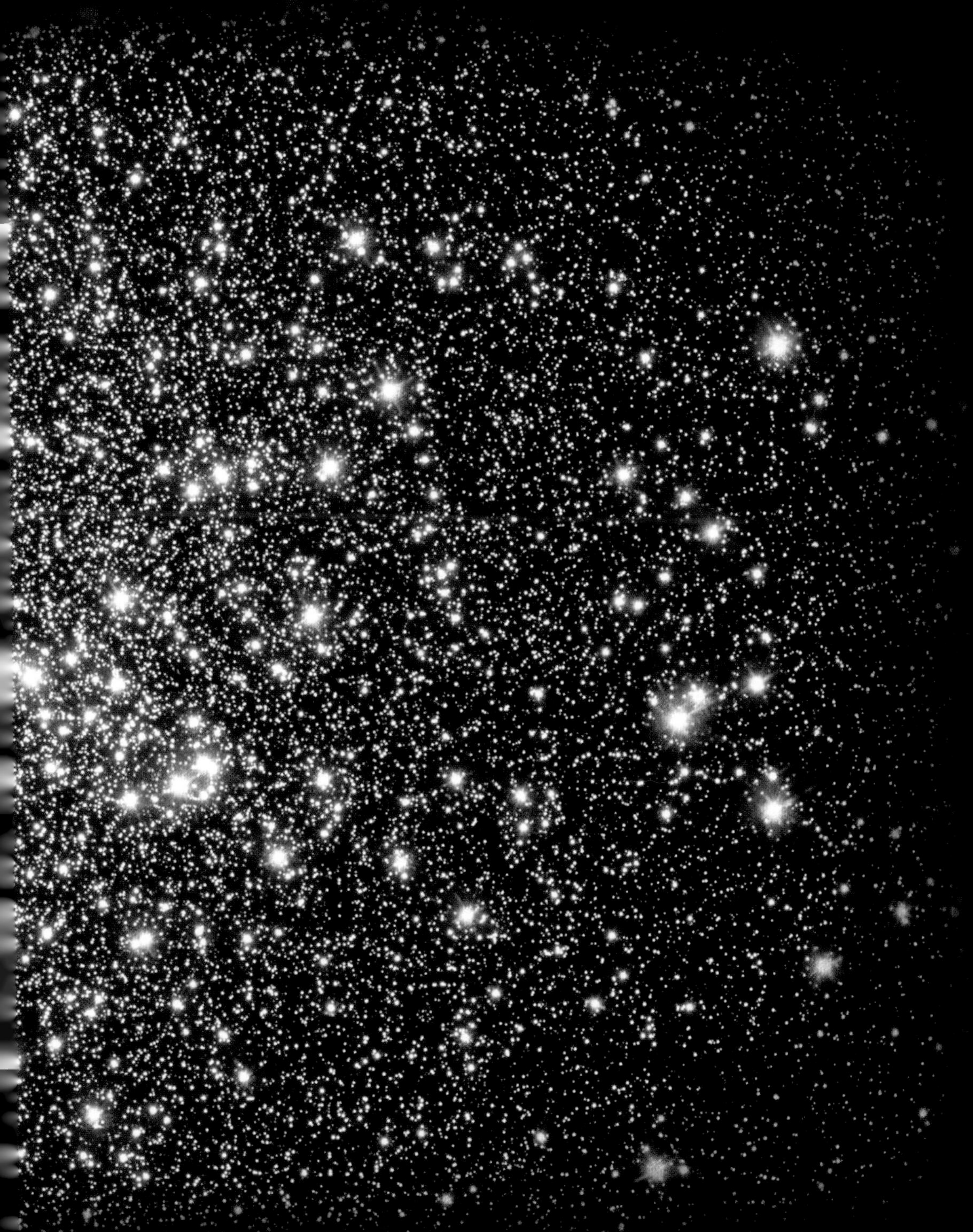

UNFORGOTTEN

Nobody knows
where they come from.
But they come.
Impossible birds
of the big sky
and the long night
with faintest whispers
and silky rustlings
no ear can hear.
They come
like a flicker
a blink
a flash
of light
no eye is sure it's seen.
Like a thought
hard to hold.
They come
to watch over
and to warm
and to mend.

But their work is not easy
and one of them is overcome
and sinks
through the night
to ground.

Weakened, it wanders
as if dreaming
resting where it can
until rest is not enough
and it comes to a stop.
There it stays
invisible to some
growing numb and stony still
until
it appears, like a statue
for all to see
casting shadows in the light.
Finally, it is given a resting place.

But before it can move no more
its plight is heeded.
And it is watched over
and warmed
and mended.
And where it goes
nobody knows.

Image Acknowledgements

USA, New York, New York City, View from Empire State Building, Night photographed by Gregor Schuster is used in the artwork on pages 12–13 courtesy of Getty Images; *Wollongong Sunrise* photographed by Stuart Starr is used in the artwork on pages 50–51, 52 courtesy of Stuart Starr; *Earth at Night 2001* [NASA/Goddard Space Flight Center Scientific Visualization Studio] is used in the artwork on pages 5, 7, 8–9, 123; *Myriad of Stars in Spiral Galaxy NGC300* [NASA and the Hubble Heritage Team (AURA/STScI)] is used in the artwork on pages 16–17; *Glittering Metropolis* [NASA, ESA, and the Hubble Heritage Team (STScI/AURA)] is used in the artwork on pages 124–125.

Details in some of the book's artwork are sourced from various archival photos. Many of these were from the Library of Congress, Prints & Photographs Division—in particular the Detroit Publishing Company Collection, HABS, National Child Labor Committee Collection, FSA-OWI Collection, Civil War Photographs, and the Gottscho-Schleisner Collection.

Further details were sourced from a collection of slides of a crossing of the Sahara Desert in 1955 taken by the author's late father, Egerton Harold Riddle.

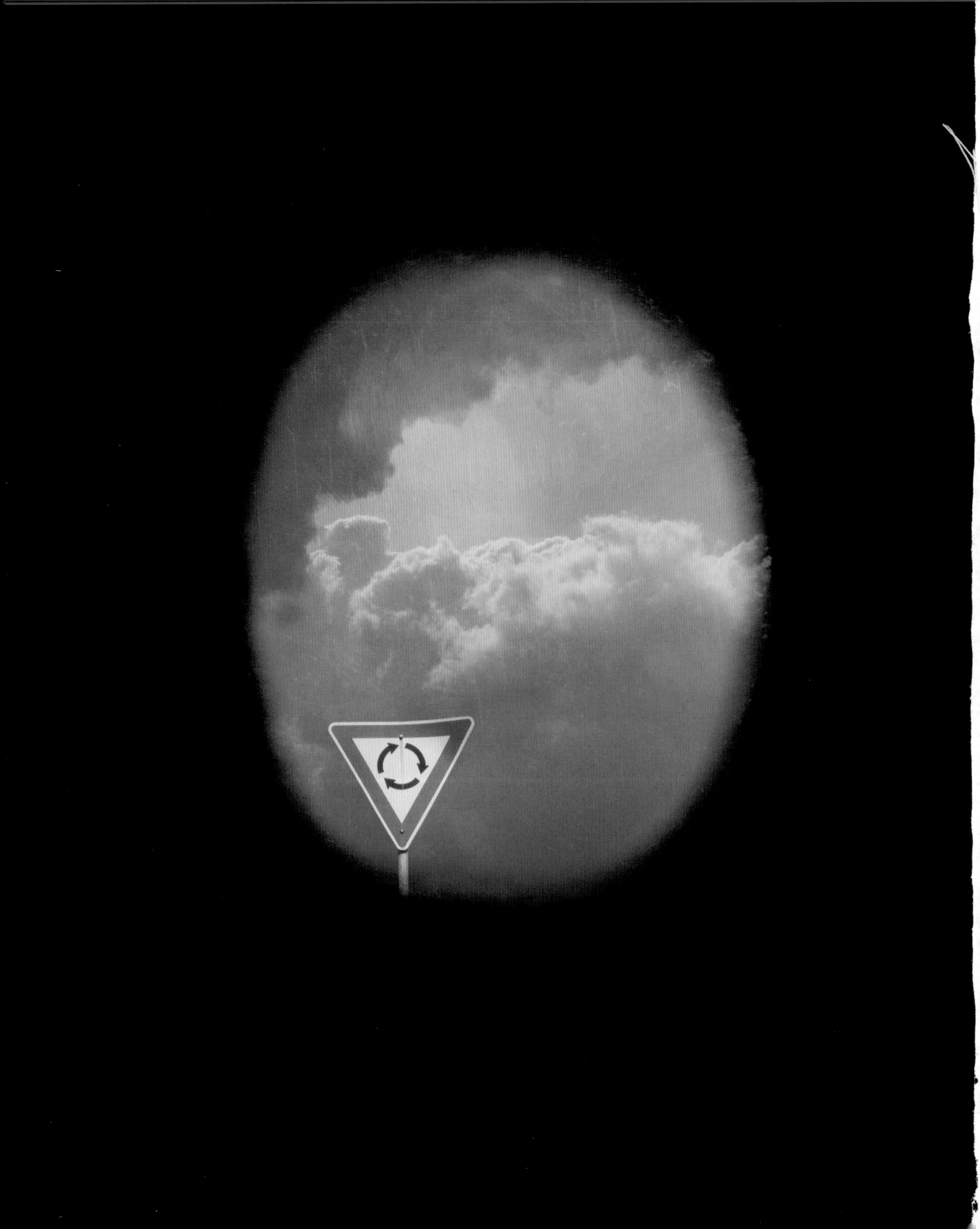

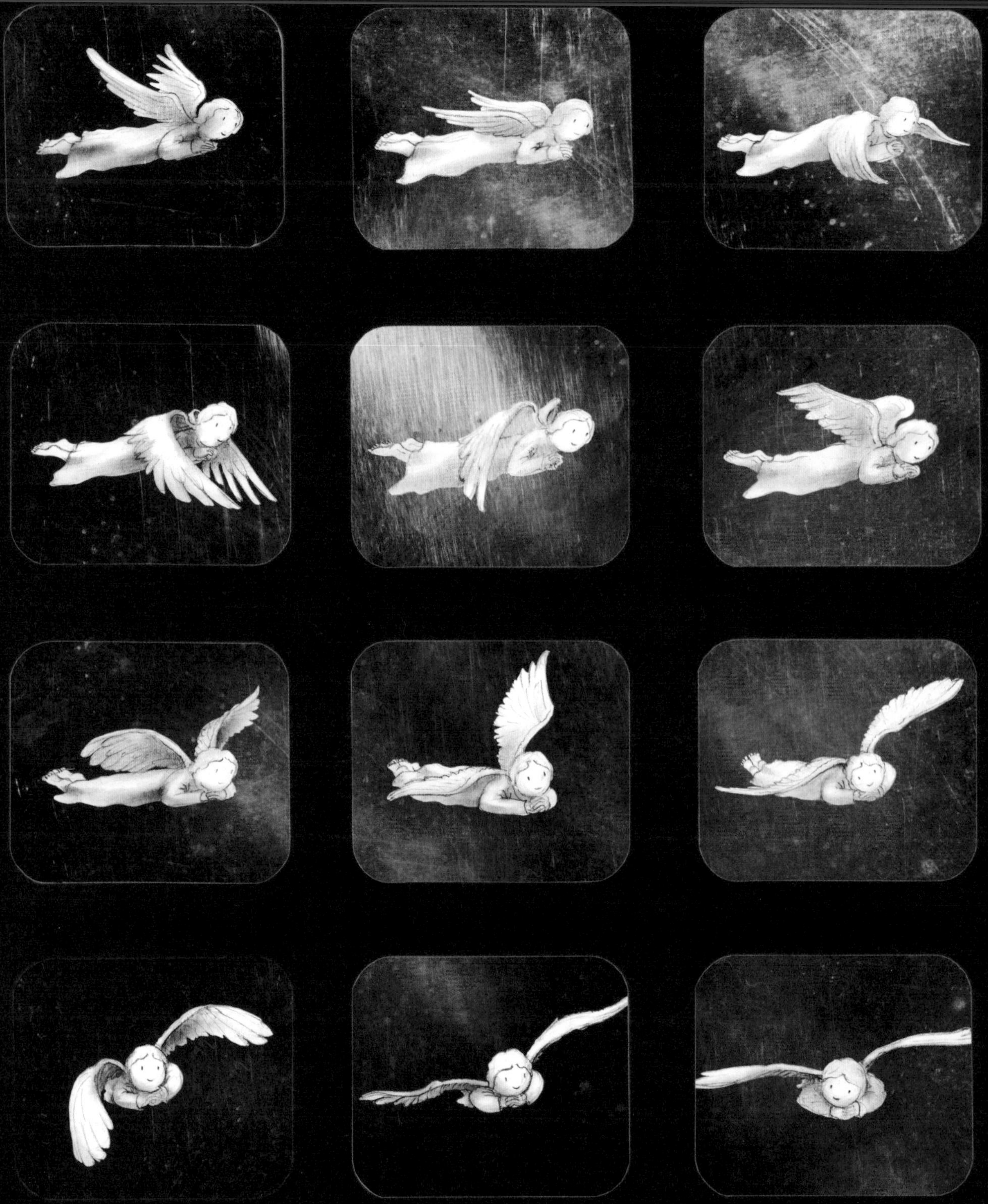